Your Space

Workbook 3

Martyn Hobbs and Julia Starr Keddle

CAMBRIDGE
UNIVERSITY PRESS

CAMBRIDGE
UNIVERSITY PRESS & ASSESSMENT

Shaftesbury Road, Cambridge CB2 8EA, United Kingdom

One Liberty Plaza, 20th Floor, New York, NY 10006, USA

477 Williamstown Road, Port Melbourne, VIC 3207, Australia

314–321, 3rd Floor, Plot 3, Splendor Forum, Jasola District Centre,
New Delhi – 110025, India

103 Penang Road, #05-06/07, Visioncrest Commercial, Singapore 238467

Cambridge University Press & Assessment is a department of the University of Cambridge.

We share the University's mission to contribute to society through the pursuit of
education, learning and research at the highest international levels of excellence.

www.cambridge.org
Information on this title: www.cambridge.org/9780521729345

© Cambridge University Press & Assessment 2012

First published 2012

20 19 18 17 16

Printed in Great Britain by Ashford Colour Press Ltd.

A catalogue record for this publication is available from the British Library

ISBN 978-0-521-72934-5 Workbook with Audio CD, Level 3
ISBN 978-0-521-72933-8 Student's Book, Level 3
ISBN 978-0-521-72935-2 Teacher's Book, Level 3
ISBN 978-0-521-72937-6 Class Audio CDs (3), Level 3

Contents

1 Complete the article with the verbs.

> take part in   listen to   give   eat   wear   ~~watch~~   go to   put up

How I celebrate Diwali – the festival of light

Hi, my name's Reena. I'm from Tividale in the centre of England. Diwali is an important festival in my culture. We celebrate for five days in November.

1 Light is important in Diwali so we ...._watch_........ fireworks outside. They're beautiful.
2 People .... decorations in their home and in shops.
3 We .... new clothes for Diwali. Girls have traditional saris.
4 We .... the Balaji temple in the morning. It's the biggest one in Europe.
5 Then we .... traditional Diwali food and special sweets. Yum!
6 Later we all .... Indian music and we dance. It's fun.
7 All the young people .... a peace parade with candles.
8 We .... presents and Diwali cards.

2 Match the celebrations from Exercise 1 with the pictures.

a 6   b   c   d
e   f   g   h

3 Write about a festival in your country.

At New Year we take part in a dragon parade. We watch fireworks.

4 💿 2 (Circle) the correct words. Then listen and check.

BEST EVER DAY

I ¹(**was watching**) / **watched** a boring TV programme last Saturday when my best friend called and invited me to celebrate his birthday. We ² **have** / **had** a great time. His mum and dad gave ³ **him** / **her** loads of money and he ⁴ **bought** / **buy** a great mobile phone – it takes amazing photos, too! Then while we ⁵ **went** / **were going** into ⁶ **town** / **school** we saw an advert for that new 3D film at the cinema – it was absolutely fantastic! After that we ⁷ **go** / **went** to the new pizzeria on the High Street and ⁸ **drank** / **ate** pizza before we got the bus home. Best day ever!

Ⓡ

Past simple and past continuous

1 Unscramble the letters to find the verbs. Then complete the table.

1 gsni ....._sing_..... 5 grbin ....
2 eahct ....._teach_.... 6 og ....
3 keta .... 7 kareb ....
4 rietw .... 8 krdin ....

Positive	Negative
1 sang	didn't sing
2	
3	
4	
5	
6	
7	
8	

2 Complete Millie's diary with the past simple form of the verbs in brackets.

Dear Diary!
Wow! What an awesome day! I ¹ ....._felt_.... (feel) so excited about visiting the Hollywood studios! Our class ² .... (meet) outside the school at 7 am (too early!) ☹. Kate ³ .... (stay) at my house the night before and we ⁴ .... (not go) to bed until after midnight so we ⁵ .... (sleep) for two hours on the bus. ☺
Hollywood is amazing! We ⁶ .... (eat) lunch in a famous restaurant. All the stars go there! Then a guide ⁷ .... (show) us round the studios. We ⁸ .... (look) in all the famous actors' rooms! After that we ⁹ .... (choose) a costume and make-up artists ¹⁰ .... (help) us to put make-up on. Before we ¹¹ .... (get) on the bus the teachers ¹² .... (take) our pictures in front of the studio cameras! That was so cool!

HOLLYWOOD

3 Reorder the words to make questions. Then write answers for you.

1 did / from / text message / who / get / you / a / yesterday / ?
Who did you get a text message from yesterday?
I got a text message from Teo yesterday.

2 write / many / you / emails / did / last / how / week / ?
....
....

3 your / go / holiday / where / last / you / did / for / ?
....
....

4 did / last / do / what / you / weekend / ?
....
....

5 last / you / what / dinner / eat / did / for / night / ?
....
....

6 lesson / was / last / yesterday / what / your / ?
....
....

7 lunch / you / have / who / did / with / yesterday / ?
....
....

8 do / last / what / birthday / did / your / you / for / ?
....
....

4 Match the expressions with the pictures of Danielle and Jessica. Then complete the sentences.

have lunch ☐   sleep 1   do their homework ☐   play tennis ☐   have breakfast ☐   study Maths ☐

| 1 | 6.30 | 2 | 7.00 | 3 | 9.30 | 4 | 13.00 | 5 | 15.00 | 6 | 18.00 |

1 At 6.30 *Danielle and Jessica were sleeping.*
2 At 7.00 ....
3 At 9.30 ....
4 At 13.00 ....
5 At 15.00 ....
6 At 18.00 ....

5 Complete the conversations with the past continuous form of the verbs in brackets.

1 **Alisha** Hi Ricky. Why .... *were* .... you .... *standing* .... (stand) outside the headteacher's office this morning?

   Ricky Mr Smith sent me because I .... (play) with my mobile phone in class.

2 **Ryan** Why didn't you answer my call last night, Max?

   Max I didn't hear the phone. I .... (listen) to music on my headphones.

3 **Lucy** What .... Jay .... (do) outside the hall at 4 o'clock, Tom?

   Tom He .... (wait) for you! You forgot!

when/while

6 ⟨Circle⟩ the correct words.

1 Maisie ⟨**was talking**⟩ / **talked** on the phone when her mum called her for dinner.

2 Poppy **was losing** / **lost** her purse while she was coming home from school.

3 We **made** / **were making** a lot of noise when the teacher came into the classroom.

4 They were walking down the street when they **were seeing** / **saw** the accident.

5 Who **did you speak** / **were you speaking** to when I saw you outside the cinema?

6 They **made** / **were making** a birthday card for Hannah when Mum came home from work.

7 The computer **crashed** / **was crashing** while we were writing the webzine.

8 We were riding our bikes in the park when Toby **was falling off** / **fell off**.

7 Complete the sentences with the correct form of the verbs in brackets.

1 Martha's mobile rang while she .... *was talking* .... (talk) to the teacher.

2 Luke was playing his guitar when one of the strings .... (break).

3 Ahmet .... (fall) over while he was playing tennis.

4 Adam and Billy were eating dinner when their favourite TV programme .... (start).

5 Alice listened to music while she .... (do) her homework.

6 The twins .... (play) chess when their dad arrived home.

7 My sister fell asleep while we .... (watch) the film.

8 We were waiting for the bus when we .... (see) Alena.

We must finish today ⊞ 1B

1 Match the interests with the websites.

Animals [8] Travel [ ] History [ ] Music [ ] Sport [ ] Film [ ] Food [ ] Shopping [ ]

Wyzzd Results

Everything

More

The web

Pages

More search tools

1 Recipes for teens Want to cook? Don't know how? Find simple fun recipes for teenagers ...

2 Past times Ancient Egypt was an ancient civilization of North Africa ...

3 Summer soon Planning a holiday next summer? Find the best on the web ...

4 CHILL OUT Downloads and videos. The best place for hip hop, rock, heavy metal ...

5 Celebrity watch The quick way to get all the news about your favourite stars ...

6 Compare prices Where to get the cheapest clothes, shoes, electrical goods ...

7 ABC Sport Find out about all the action. Football, tennis, basketball ...

8 Wildlife finder The place where you can find your favourite animals ... photos, maps, information ...

2 Find the words in the word square.

monitor · cursor · upload · bookmark · download · printer · comment · mouse · post · website · screen · blog

A	B	D	U	P	L	O	A	D	M
D	O	W	N	L	O	A	D	R	O
P	O	E	C	U	R	S	O	R	N
R	K	B	Z	P	B	L	O	G	I
I	M	S	C	O	M	M	E	N	T
N	A	I	D	S	B	O	C	F	O
T	R	T	P	T	H	U	I	K	R
E	K	E	O	J	A	S	P	B	N
R	M	T	S	C	R	E	E	N	D

Chat zone

3 Complete the conversations with the expressions. Then listen and check.

It's hilarious!   the whole time   It was so embarrassing!   I'm not allowed to

1 Teo Was Chrissie talking on her mobile during the film?
Ella Yes, and everyone was looking at us.
....

2 Erin Are you coming to the disco on Saturday, Zoe?
Zoe Mum says .... go.

3 Alice Did you have fun on the school trip?
Emma Yes, we were laughing and singing ....

4 Jack Did you watch the comedy film on TV last night?
Ryan Yes, and I couldn't stop laughing.
....

must / have to

1 Look at the pictures. Complete the rules with *must* or *mustn't*.

1 **30** You ___mustn't___ drive fast.

2 SILENCE You _____ be quiet.

3 You _____ eat or drink here.

4 You _____ fasten your seatbelt.

5 You _____ feed the ducks.

6 No Parking You _____ park here.

2 Ellie is thinking about what she must do. Match the actions with the pictures. Then write sentences.

write an email to Zoe ☐   tidy my room [1]

phone Callum ☐   cook dinner ☐

buy tickets for the Beyoncé concert ☐

do my homework ☐   buy some jeans ☐

practise the guitar ☐

1 I must tidy my room.
2 I _____
3 I _____
4 I _____
5 I _____
6 I _____
7 I _____
8 I _____

3 Write about what you and your family must do this weekend.

_____
_____
_____
_____

4 Complete the conversation with the correct form of *have to*.

Chrissie   Lauren, [1]___do you have to___ get up before 7 am every day?

Lauren   Yes, I [2]_____ . It's awful!

Chrissie   And [3]_____ your mum _____ work on Saturday?

Lauren   No, she [4]_____ . She only works part-time.

Chrissie   [5]_____ your older brother _____ go to bed before midnight on Saturday?

Lauren   No, he [6]_____ . It's not fair! I always [7]_____ be in bed by 10 pm!

Chrissie   And [8]_____ he _____ help your mum and dad with the housework?

Lauren   No, he [9]_____ . And it's awful when I [10]_____ go into his room. What a mess!

5 Read the email from Molly to Megan. Complete the sentences with *had to* or *didn't have to*.

To: Megan
From: Molly

Dear Megan,

I'm so glad Mum's home! She ¹ _had to_ stay in hospital for five days so I ² .... take my brothers, Billy and Sam, to school every day.
I ³ .... cook dinner because Auntie Carla did that every evening but I ⁴ .... make sandwiches for our lunches every day.
The worst thing was the ironing! I ⁵ .... iron all our clothes because Dad was at work from 8 am until 6 pm and didn't have time! He ⁶ .... clean the house and do the washing at the weekend.
We were so unlucky! Dad's car wasn't working so we ⁷ .... catch the train to school every morning. But we ⁸ .... wait very long – there was a train every five minutes. One good thing happened! When I told the teacher that Mum was in hospital she said I ⁹ .... do my homework but I ¹⁰ .... relax when Billy and Sam went to bed!
Write to me soon.
Love,

Molly

Communication

4 Complete the conversations. Then listen and check.

| problem | not allowed | mobile | sorry | lessons | outside | can | course | break | allowed | lunch | ~~have to~~ |

A
Daisy Are you a new student? Do you need any help?
Sophie Yes, please. Do you ¹ _have to_ eat in the canteen?
Daisy No, you can bring your ² .... from home.
Sophie Are you ³ .... to go to the toilet during the lesson?
Daisy Yes, you are.
Sophie Can I use my ⁴ .... at school?
Daisy Of ⁵ .... you can, but you must switch it off during the ⁶ ....

B
Beth Excuse me, Sir. ⁷ .... I open the window?
Teacher Of course you can.
Emma Can we have a ⁸ .... now?
Teacher Sure. No ⁹ ....
Sophie Are we allowed to go ¹⁰ .... during the break?
Teacher No, I'm ¹¹ .... , you can't. It's ¹² ....
Beth What a pity!

Reading

Glastonbury Festival

– it started so small and got so big!

Imagine having a party and inviting your favourite bands and singers to perform! Well, every year in June there is a five-day party at Glastonbury in the south-west of England. It's the world's biggest open-air music festival!

How it started

In 1970, a farmer called Michael Eavis decided to organise a music festival on his farm. Before that the small town of Glastonbury was only famous for its legends about King Arthur. In that first year 1,500 people paid £1 each to listen to a few bands. It was a small festival and Michael gave them free milk.

The 21st century festival

Nowadays 'Glasto' is very big and Michael's daughter, Emily, helps him with the festival. There are about 400 performances and 80 different stages. And it isn't just about music. There are art and dance shows, and you can go to the circus, the theatre or the cinema and visit hundreds of shops, restaurants and cafés. Performers include U2, Dizzee Rascal and Lily Allen.

Life at the festival

When the tickets go on sale people have to be very quick! In 2011, a five-day ticket cost £195 – but all 150,000 tickets sold out in four hours. Young people come with their friends, and many families come with their children and teenagers. Most festival-goers camp – there are thousands of tents and it's easy to get lost! People dress up in silly costumes and there are lots of multicoloured flags. Sometimes it rains a lot – Glastonbury is famous for its mud! But it's always fun. And if you can't go, you can always watch the concerts on TV.

After the festival

At the end of the festival there is lots of rubbish. 500 staff take two weeks to clean up the 1,650 tonnes of rubbish, including thousands of cans and bottles, and they recycle about 50% of it. For the rest of the year Michael's cows live on the festival fields!

1 Read the article and match the numbers with the words and phrases.

1 one thousand, five hundred   a stages
2 four hundred   b shops, restaurants and cafés
3 eighty   c festival tickets in 2011
4 hundreds   d people at the festival in 1970
5 one hundred and fifty thousand   e tonnes of rubbish
6 one thousand, six hundred and fifty   f performances

2 Read the article again. Are the sentences true (*T*) or false (*F*)?

1 The Glastonbury Festival lasts five days and is in June. ...T...
2 Michael Eavis started the festival in 2010. ....
3 The first festival-goers paid £1 for their tickets. ....
4 You can watch bands and films, dance, eat, buy things and camp at the festival. ....
5 It is always sunny during the Glastonbury Festival. ....
6 Visitors take all their rubbish home with them. ....

Listening

3 ◯ 5 **Listen and match the people with their worst and best moments.**

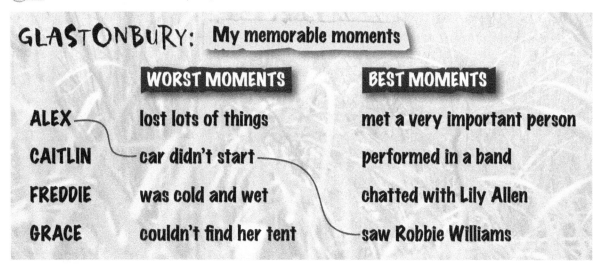

GLASTONBURY: My memorable moments

WORST MOMENTS

BEST MOMENTS

ALEX — lost lots of things   met a very important person

CAITLIN — car didn't start —   performed in a band

FREDDIE   was cold and wet   chatted with Lily Allen

GRACE   couldn't find her tent — saw Robbie Williams

Writing

4 **Write a description of a festival, a show or a sporting event you have taken part in. Include this information:**

- what it was
- when and where it was
- what you did and saw there
- your opinion

Writing focus

When you write about past events, check your past simple verbs. Are they regular or irregular?

Your progress

Look at Student's Book Unit 1. Circle: 😦 = not very well 🙂 = quite well 😄 = very well

I can talk about things I was doing yesterday.	😦 🙂 😄	p9
I can understand information about websites.	😦 🙂 😄	p12
I can understand and talk about duties and rules.	😦 🙂 😄	p13
I can have a conversation about everyday life and indicate when I am following.	😦 🙂 😄	p16
I can read an article about festivals and understand the main points.	😦 🙂 😄	p17
I can ask about rules and understand information about a gym.	😦 🙂 😄	p108

Your project: my top festival

- Write four short paragraphs about your favourite festival in your country or region.

  the festival: why and where it happens

  description: what happens, what you eat, how you celebrate, etc.

  a story: what I or my family did last time we had the festival

  my opinion: what I like about the festival

- Draw pictures or find photos and make a poster.

1 Unscramble the letters and label the pictures.

> xtet skobo   snep dan lipsnec   DDV   vincetirate hewit daorb   ~~DC~~
>
> shanpeehod   knoostobe   thiwe darob   metcroup   keds

1 ....CD...........

2 ...c....................

3 ..p...................

4 ...d...................

5 ...h...................

6 ...D...................

7 ...i...................

8 ...t...................

9 ...w...................

10 ...n...................

2 Complete the sentences with the words from Exercise 1.

1 I don't like writing on the ..white board.. I've got very bad handwriting!

2 I always sit at the same .... next to the window. I sometimes look outside and dream!

3 I keep my .... in the pocket of my school bag. I haven't got a proper container for them.

4 I really like the .... We can see pictures from the book, do exercises together, watch a video and go on the internet. And it's all in the same place!

5 I use lots of different .... I have one for vocabulary, another one for grammar, and another one for my English diary.

6 I sometimes listen to music on a .... but I prefer my mp3 player.

7 I've got a .... but it's quite slow. I sometimes use my dad's one. It's new and a lot faster!

8 I have to carry lots of .... for different subjects in my school bag. They're very heavy!

9 I watched a great .... yesterday after school. It was a funny film about a school.

10 I often listen to music and stories on my .... I can hear everything very clearly but other people can't!

will/won't • definitely/probably

1 (Circle) the correct form.

1 Chill out! History's your best subject. You (**will**)/ **won't** pass the test.

2 It's really cold. I think it **will** / **won't** snow tonight.

3 You didn't finish your project. The teacher definitely **will** / **won't** be pleased.

4 Ben really likes you. I'm sure he **will** / **won't** invite you to his party.

5 Don't worry, you **will** / **won't** miss the bus. It's only 7.30.

6 I tidied my room yesterday afternoon. Mum **will** / **won't** believe it!

7 Megan loves Beyoncé so she **will** / **won't** definitely like this CD.

8 Viktor's sick. He **will** / **won't** be at school today.

2 Write sentences with *will* and *won't*.

1 They / not find / the CD
   They won't find the CD.

2 It / not rain / this evening

3 She / go to school / by bus / tomorrow

4 Lukas / probably help you / with your homework

5 Pippa / not move / home

6 They / definitely like / the film

7 I think / we / finish / our project / today

8 You / not get / tickets / for the concert

3 Complete Alice's essay with *will* or *won't* and the verbs in brackets.

The year 3000

What **1** ..will.. the world ..be.. (be) like for teenagers in the year 3000?
I think life **2** .... (not be) very different from today. Kids in the future **3** .... (have to) do too much homework and parents **4** .... (tell) them to be polite and tidy their rooms. Teachers **5** .... (shout) at them when they fail a test or when they don't do their homework. Parents **6** .... (not want) to spend money on the coolest trainers and they definitely **7** .... (not allow) their kids to go to bed late.
Life isn't easy for a teenager now and it **8** .... (continue) to be difficult in the year 3000!

4 Complete the conversation with the expressions.

> we'll have   she will   you'll win   will help
> ~~it'll be~~   it'll rain   it won't   we'll take

Lauren Hi, Harry! You're looking happy!

Harry Yeah! I think **1** _it'll be_ sunny tomorrow for our football tournament.

Lauren Are you sure? I think **2** .... in the afternoon.

Harry No, **3** .... , **4** .... perfect weather all day.

Lauren That's great news. **5** .... a picnic and have it after the match. I'm sure Sofia **6** .... me. What do you think?

Harry Of course **7** .... Then we can celebrate our team's victory.

Lauren The other team's very good, Harry. Are you sure **8** .... ?

Harry Absolutely. We're the best!

5 Write questions. Then answer for you.

1 you / send lots of text messages / this afternoon
Will you send lots of text messages this afternoon? Yes, I will.

2 it / rain tonight

....

3 you / get up early / tomorrow

....

4 your parents / let you go to a party / on Saturday night

....

5 you / hang out with your friends / this weekend

....

6 you / tidy your room / soon

....

7 you / study English / next year

....

8 you / travel to lots of countries / in the future

....

6 Write questions with the verbs and complete the short answers.

be enjoy go pass win ~~spend~~ make

1 *Will they spend* New Year at home?
Yes, *they will* . They never go away at New Year.

2 .... the Geography exam?
No, ... He doesn't study enough.

3 .... the school play?
Yes, ... She always enjoys them!

4 .... the sports tournament this year?
No, ... They aren't as good as the other team.

5 .... ready for the concert tomorrow?
No, ... He can't play all the music.

6 .... friends in her new school?
Yes, ... She's very friendly.

7 .... on holiday to Spain?
Yes, ... We go there every year.

7 Write sentences with *will* or *may/might* and one of the verbs.

surf post take stay buy tidy ~~go~~

1 **Mat** What are you doing this weekend, Sam?
Sam I'm not sure. I *may go* to the disco on Saturday.

2 **Jack** What are you doing after school, Rob?
Rob I think I .... at school and go to the music club.

3 **Tom** What will you do on Sunday?
Emma I don't know. I .... some photos of the city centre for our project.

4 **Ethan** What are you doing this evening, Evie?
Evie I'm not sure. I .... a message on my blog.

5 **Megan** What will you do at the weekend, Jodi?
Jodi I .... my room – it's a mess!

6 **Lauren** I don't know what I want to do this evening.
Jessica I do! I .... the web for our research project.

7 **Darren** I'm buying the new Beyoncé CD this weekend.
Trisha She's not my favourite but I .... it too. I've heard it's good.

1 Unscramble the letters and complete the crossword.

1 TEER SUOEH

2 GRENEY–NIVAGS

13 GLITH BBLU

3 NEGER OROF

4 NIDW BERUNIT

5 RAEWT NAKT

6 SRALO NELAP

7 POSTCOM

10 NIB

8 CECNGYILR

11 INB

12 AGEBELETV

9 NRADEG

2 Choose the correct bin for recycling these things.

an empty cola can [2]   an old photo [ ]   potato peel [ ]   a yoghurt pot [ ]   a plastic bag [ ]
printing paper [ ]   a plastic water bottle [ ]   rice [ ]   a banana skin [ ]   a cereal packet [ ]
a magazine [ ]   an empty can of tomatoes [ ]

1 PAPER & CARDBOARD

2 METAL

3 GLASS

4 FOOD

5 PLASTIC

3 Write about three things you recycled last week.

Chat zone

6 Complete the conversations with the expressions. Then listen and check.

Really?   What a pain!   No worries.

1 **Robbie**   Thanks for giving me the name of that website – it was so useful!

  Liam   ....

2 **Erin**   Mum and Dad are buying me a new computer for my birthday.

  Ryan   .... That's so cool!

3 **Jacob**   ....
    I left my homework at home!

  Damian   You'll have to go and get it!

will for offers, promises and decisions

1 Match 1–6 with a–f.

1 Sorry I failed the test, Mum.
2 I'm so tired!
3 Your plane arrives very late.
4 Those jeans are too expensive.
5 Are you collecting for charity?
6 I'm really hungry.

a I'll get a snack in the break! ☐
b I'll try a cheaper shop. ☐
c I'll give you some money. ☐
d I'll study more next time. ☐ 1
e I'll meet you at the airport. ☐
f I'll go to bed early. ☐

2 Look at the pictures and write sentences.

1 Cheer up, Sophie! I / cook / your / favourite dinner!
Cheer up, Sophie! I'll cook your favourite dinner!

2 Look at those black clouds! I / take / my umbrella!

....

....

3 We need more photos for our project. I / try / that new website tonight.

....

....

4 I don't like catching the bus. I / ride / my bike this morning!

....

....

5 You've got a very high temperature, Brandon! I / call / the doctor.

....

....

6 I can never dance well at the disco. I / take / dance lessons!

....

....

Present continuous and *going to*

3 Look at Maisie's diary for next week. Write sentences using the present continuous.

Mon	post new message on my blog
Tues	shop with Megan for clothes
Wed	study for Maths test
Thurs	watch first episode of new reality TV show!
Fri	collect money in town centre for earthquake victims
Sat	wear new clothes to disco
Sun	run in school marathon

1 On Monday she's posting a new message on her blog.

4 Complete the conversation with the present continuous form of the verbs.

swim sing go run meet play ~~watch~~

Chloe Hi, Jacob! ¹ _Are_ you _watching_ the football match on TV tonight?

Jacob No, I'm not. I don't really like football. I ² .... Ali in the town centre and we ³ .... to the new Sports Club they opened on Regent Street last week.

Chloe No way! I'd love to go there!

Jacob Come along too! We ⁴ .... at 5 o'clock and then we ⁵ .... tennis until 7 o'clock.

Chloe I'll invite Katie and we can play together!

Jacob That's a brilliant idea! ⁶ .... you .... in the school marathon on Sunday morning?

Chloe Yes, I am and I ⁷ .... in the school concert on Sunday evening! I'll be asleep in class on Monday!

5 Write sentences about your plans this week.

1 Tonight I ....

2 After school I ....

3 This week I ....

4 Tomorrow I'm meeting ....

5 At the weekend I'm ....

6 Complete the conversation with the correct form of the verbs in brackets.

Rosie I made loads of New Year's resolutions this year, Ellie. What about you?

Ellie Well, I ¹ _'m going to work_ (work) much harder at school – we've got important exams this summer! Mum and Dad ² .... (buy) me a new computer – my old one's so slow – and I ³ .... (use) it for homework projects and research. How about you, Rosie? What ⁴ .... you .... (do) this year?

Rosie Well, I'm ⁵ .... (not argue) with my little brother so much and I ⁶ .... (not watch) so much TV. I ⁷ .... (not be) so shy. I ⁸ .... (ask) the Drama teacher if I can be in the school play in June.

Ellie Wow, Rosie! That's fantastic! I want to be in the school play, too!

7 Write five resolutions for you.

1 (food) ....

2 (sport) ....

3 (work) ....

4 (school) ....

5 (hobbies) ....

Communication

7 Look at the pictures and complete the conversation. Then listen and check.

foreground background looks look like left ~~describe~~ else middle think

Tina Can you ¹ _describe_ your favourite photo?

Alex Sure! In the ² .... , I can see trees and buildings. In the ³ .... of the picture, I can see some people.

Tina What are they doing?

Alex They're sitting on the grass and they're looking at the view. I ⁴ .... they're having a nice time.

Tina What ⁵ .... can you see?

Alex In the ⁶ .... , there's a girl on the ⁷ .... She's lying on the grass and she's reading a book. She ⁸ .... really interested in it.

Tina What does she ⁹ .... ?

Alex She's got long brown hair. You know, I really like this photo. It reminds me of a really happy day!

Reading

1 Read the article and write the headings above the paragraphs.

Clothes Working Sleeping Gravity Food Relaxing ~~Recycling~~

Life on the International Space Station

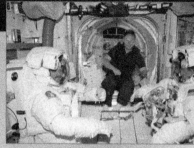

Imagine living with 16 sunrises and sunsets every day – 400 km above the Earth! Strange? Well, for the astronauts on the International Space Station it's normal! Between two and 13 astronauts from 16 nations live on the space station together for about six months.

1 ...... *Recycling* ......

It's very expensive to carry things to the space station so the station is as 'green' as possible! They recycle water and air, re-use rubbish and use solar energy. Complex systems control life on the station and provide clean water and oxygen.

2 ....

Astronauts eat normal food. There is soup, meat, vegetables, nuts, cereals, cakes and biscuits. And they drink coffee, tea, orange juice or lemonade. The food is either ready-to-eat, or dried so they have to add water. And they can heat their meals in an oven.

3 ....

In space there is no gravity so everyday activities become more difficult. Astronauts have to use special trays and a belt to stay in their seats. And they use salt and pepper in liquid form – because real salt and pepper float away!

4 ....

Inside the station they wear shirts or T-shirts, shorts or trousers, sweaters and trainers. The crew can't wash their clothes, so they don't change very often! They wear special space suits when they work outside the station, and orange suits for their journeys.

5 ....

Sleeping can be difficult because it is not dark for long. The cabins are very small with no beds! With no gravity, the astronauts' sleeping bags are attached to the walls on a hook! They sleep for about five or six hours.

6 ....

The astronauts do research into biology, medicine, astronomy and gravity. They take part in experiments about how their bodies change in space. They also help to maintain and build the station.

7 ....

Life in space is not just work! The crew enjoy looking at Earth out of the windows, listening to music, playing computer games and cards, watching films, reading, and talking to their families. And each day they also keep fit in the gym.

2 Read the article again and answer the questions.

1 Why is the space station 'green'?

2 What are some problems of life in the station?

3 Where do the astronauts sleep?

4 What work do they do?

3 Complete the spidergram with words from the article. Then draw two spidergrams for *food* and *free time* and complete them.

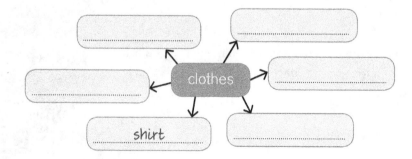

clothes

shirt

Listening

4 🔘 **8** Listen to an interview with Angela Lopez, an astronaut at the International Space Station. Complete the activities with the times and put them in the correct order.

a did some exercise ☐

b had lunch at .... ☐

c woke up at ...6 am... 1

d had dinner at .... ☐

e had a quick shower ☐

f free time ☐

g went to bed at .... ☐

h had a morning meeting at .... ☐

i finished work at .... ☐

j had another meeting ☐

5 🔘 **8** Listen again and (circle) the correct answers.

1 Did you enjoy your time in space? (yes) / no

2 What's it like on the space station? **horrible / fun**

3 What was your job? **checking water safety / cleaning the station**

4 What about the weekend?

Friday: **watching TV / watching movies**   Saturday: **cleaning / chatting**

Sunday: **talking with family / watching movies**

5 What was the best thing? **cleaning the windows / looking out of the windows**

Writing

6 **Write about the things you did last week.**

- what you did during the week (school, sport, clubs)
- what you did at the weekend (family activities, chores, free time activities)
- what you liked best

> **Writing focus**
>
> Why not keep an English diary or blog? Write a short paragraph each week. It will help improve your English.

Your progress

Look at Student's Book Unit 2. Circle: ☹ = **not very well** ☺ = **quite well** 😎 = **very well**

I can read and understand an article about the future.	☹ ☺ 😎 p19
I can talk about the future, make plans and make predictions.	☹ ☺ 😎 p19 p20 p23
I can read an article about the environment and understand the main points.	☹ ☺ 😎 p26
I can listen and understand students talking about the future.	☹ ☺ 😎 p27
I can write a comment responding to an article and give my opinion.	☹ ☺ 😎 p27
I can describe a picture and ask for more details about the picture.	☹ ☺ 😎 p109

Your project: my guide to a greener life

- Think of five tips for how to live a greener life. Be creative!
  Organise a swap day. Bring in things to swap.
- Find information and pictures from the internet or magazines.
- Write advice for each tip.
- Make a poster or a computer presentation.
- Present your guide to the class.

1 Complete the sentences with the activities.

go-karting   rock climbing   ~~surfing~~   trampolining   ice skating
scuba diving   skiing   canoeing   skateboarding   mountain biking

---

http://yourspace.cambridge.org

1 I go ....surfing.... a lot in the summer. There are great beaches and lots of big waves here in Australia. I've got a surfboard and a wetsuit. **floyd**

2 My friends come round to my house and we do .... in my garden. I love jumping really high! **sunny**

3 I love going .... at the circuit. It's fun going fast! Sometimes I win a race. **speeder**

4 I go .... in the skate park with my friends. My skateboard is old so I'm saving to buy a new one. **phoenix**

5 My family and I go .... in the mountains when there's lots of snow. I'm quite good at it, and I don't fall over very often! **pink**

6 I like going .... in the summer with my friends. I love being high in the mountains. It's a challenge, and you have to be very careful. **neo**

7 Our family go .... in the countryside at the weekend. It's fun being on wheels – unless you get a flat tyre! **darkstar**

8 I go .... twice a week at the ice rink. It's a bit like dancing and it's good for keeping fit. I am practising for a competition. **hunnybear**

9 We live near a river, not the sea. So I go .... I love being with my friends on the water. It's fun and I get fit. **gollum**

10 I love going .... It's very exciting to swim underwater and see lots of unusual fish. **ice**

2 Write a comment about your favourite activity for the website. Invent a username!

Chat zone

9 Complete the conversations with the expressions. Then listen and check.

That's all.   Very funny!   ... believe it or not.
I can't stand ...

1 **Tom**   I didn't do my Maths homework. Mrs Scott is going to be really angry.
  Sam   Tell her you did it, but your dog ate it!
  Tom   ....

2 **Lauren**   Are you coming to the cinema with us?
  Simon   No, I'm not. .... watching horror films!

3 **Alex**   Do you want to watch TV with us?
  Daisy   Watching TV isn't the only way to relax in the evening, ...

4 **Stevie**   Have you done much sport, Darren?
  Darren   A bit of football and tennis. ....

Present perfect

1 Write the past participles of the regular and irregular verbs.

1 find .... *found* ....
2 live ....
3 work ....
4 look ....
5 study ....
6 eat ....
7 wait ....
8 hurry ....
9 bring ....
10 swim ....
11 pay ....
12 sell ....

2 Complete the sentences with the present perfect form of the verbs.

> raise do dive swim
> climb fly sleep ~~help~~

1 Owen *has helped* old people in his town.
2 Molly .... a tree.
3 We .... from a board.
4 The school .... loads of money for charity.
5 Irina and Emily .... in a tent.
6 Our cousins .... rock climbing.
7 They .... in a lake.
8 My friends .... in a plane.

3 Write about the things Ruby and Sara have done in the holidays.

	Ruby	Sara
1 swim in the sea	✓	
2 play beach volleyball	✓	✓
3 send postcards	✓	
4 sail in a boat	✓	✓
5 sunbathe on the beach		✓
6 visit a theme park		✓

1 Only Ruby has swum in the sea.
2 They have both played beach volleyball.

4 Complete the sentences with the negative form of the present perfect.

1 We *haven't finished* (not finish) the test. Can we have 20 minutes more?
2 Bethany .... (not see) that film. She'll really enjoy it!
3 Our class .... (not study) Spanish before.
4 The teacher .... (not give) us any homework. Hurray!
5 Harry and Bruno .... (not arrive) in time for class again!
6 Mum .... (not cook) burger and chips this week.

5 Look at the pictures and write about what you have/haven't done in your life.

ride a bike   cook pasta   play football

surf the web   ride a horse   win a prize

ski   play the guitar   write a blog

1 I've ridden a bike.

6 Complete Jessica's blog about New York with the correct form of the verbs.

spend	eat	take	~~live~~
climb	be	visit	see

Hi guys!

My name's Jessica and I **1** 've lived in the Big Apple all my life!
I **2** _____ three shows on Broadway and Mum's taking me to another for my birthday next month. New York has some amazing clubs but I **3** _____ to them yet because I'm only 15! I **4** _____ to the top of the Empire State Building and I **5** _____ a boat to Ellis Island – I love being a tourist!
I **6** _____ all the important art galleries – the Guggenheim's my favorite. The food in my city is fantastic. I **7** _____ in some really cool restaurants. If you **8** _____ time in my city yet, come and visit soon!

7 Write questions and short answers.

1 Ryan / win / a competition? (✗)
Has Ryan won a competition?
No, he hasn't.

2 they / raise / money for charity? (✓)
_____
_____

3 you / finish / your homework? (✗)
_____
_____

4 they / see / the new science-fiction film? (✗)
_____
_____

5 Jessica / invite / you to her party? (✓)
_____
_____

6 the magazine / publish / your photos? (✓)
_____
_____

8 Complete the sentences with *been* or *gone*.

1

Alex Where's Dean? I need his help.

Jo He's _____ gone _____ to the dentist's.

2

Mum's _____ to Paris. I hope she'll buy me a present!

3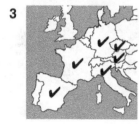

We love travelling! We've _____ to six countries in Europe.

4

Camila has _____ to see the new film. She loved it!

5

Matt and Damian have _____ to see The X Factor. It finishes at 11 o'clock tonight.

6

Dan Hi, Dad. Have you seen Mum?

Dad She's _____ to the shops.

1 Unscramble the letters and label the pictures.

~~TSRIF IAD TIK~~	SCEINT LELNEPERT	CHROT

NSU ARECM	GOKNOIC SOTEV	SCETAHM	APM

SASMOCP	PEELINGS GAB	OWLPIL

1 first aid kit   2 ....   3 ....   4 ....   5 ....

6 ....   7 ....   8 ....   9 ....   10 ....

2 Match the items from Exercise 1 with the descriptions.

1 It's a sort of picture. You use it to find directions in a new place. .... map ....

2 You use this stuff when there are a lot of insects. ....

3 You use this bag to sleep in when you are in a tent. ....

4 These sticks come in a small box. You use them to start a fire. ....

5 This small gadget helps you find North. ....

6 You use this for your head when you sleep. It's comfortable. ....

7 This is useful for cooking on when you are camping. ....

8 This cream protects your skin on a sunny day. ....

9 It uses batteries. You use it to see at night. ....

10 You use the medicine in this box if you have an accident. ....

Present perfect with *for/since*

1 Complete the time expressions with *for* or *since*.

1 ......*since*...... nine o'clock
2 .... two hours
3 .... a few minutes
4 .... December
5 .... six weeks
6 .... yesterday
7 .... last year
8 .... a month
9 .... Tuesday
10 .... a long time

2 Complete the sentences with *for* or *since*.

1 Anna's ridden horses ......*for*...... three years.
2 I haven't listened to my mp3 player .... last weekend.
3 Maisie hasn't visited her gran .... six months.
4 They haven't listened to the radio .... years.
5 Boris hasn't ridden his bike .... he had the accident.
6 Billy and Tom have played tennis .... they were 12.

3 Write negative sentences about you with *for* and *since*.

1 not swim
   I haven't swum for two months.
2 not study Science
   ....
3 not have a holiday
   ....
4 not send a text message
   ....
5 not watch a film
   ....
6 not read a magazine
   ....
7 not go shopping
   ....
8 not cycle to school
   ....

4 Complete the interview with *for* or *since* and the correct form of the verbs.

Owen Hi, Nicole. Can I ask you some questions for the class survey?
Nicole Sure, go ahead.
Owen Have you got a best friend?
Nicole Yes, I have. ¹ *I / know Noah / I started school*
I've known Noah since I started school.
Owen Have you ever seen a musical?
Nicole Yes, but not recently. ² *I / not see a musical / three years* ....

Owen Have you ever played in the school band?
Nicole No, I haven't. ³ *But I / want to play / a long time* ....

Owen Have you ever written a story?
Nicole Yeah. ⁴ *I / write stories / I was ten years old* ....

Owen Wow, that's really cool! Have you ever worked with the web team?
Nicole Yes, I have! ⁵ *I / work with the web team / September* ....

I organise all the photos.
Owen Have you ever played in a school sports team?
Nicole I certainly have. ⁶ *I / play for the school basketball team / six months* ....

We won our last match!

Present perfect and past simple

5 Complete the email with the present perfect or past simple form of the verbs in brackets.

To: Marta

From: Kirsty

Hi, Marta!

I'm so glad we're going to be e-pals. So, what can I tell you about me?

I ¹ _____was_____ (be) born in Manchester. ² _Have you ever been_ (you / ever be) there? It's a really cool city with lots of concerts – I ³ _____ (see) Beyoncé last week.

It also has my favourite football team, Manchester United. I ⁴ _____ (buy) a Manchester United football scarf last summer and I ⁵ _____ (see) all their matches since August!

I ⁶ _____ (travel) a lot because I've got relatives in the United States and Australia. Last summer we ⁷ _____ (go) to Sydney to stay with my uncle and I ⁸ _____ (try) surfing on Bondi Beach – it was amazing! We did loads of fabulous things. We went swimming with dolphins and that really was the coolest thing I ⁹ _____ (ever do) in my entire life! ¹⁰ _____ (you / ever do) that? What's the best thing you've ever done?

Write soon,

Love Kirsty

Communication

🔊 10 Complete the conversations. Then listen and check.

good	let's	agree	what	take	don't	better	should	~~raise~~	going	shall	sure

A

Kerri How can we ¹ ____raise____ funds for the people in the earthquake disaster?

Grant I'm not ² _____ .

Mel ³ _____ collect money on Saturday morning.

Kerri I don't ⁴ _____ . I think Saturday afternoon is ⁵ _____ .

Grant I agree.

B

Ricky What shall we ⁶ _____ on our picnic?

Daniel Let's take pizza and chips.

Natalie I ⁷ _____ think that's a very ⁸ _____ idea. They will be cold.

Ricky ⁹ _____ we take chicken and fruit juice? ¹⁰ _____ do you think?

Daniel That's a good idea.

Natalie We ¹¹ _____ take sandwiches and cake, too.

Ricky I agree. So, we're ¹² _____ to take chicken, fruit juice, sandwiches and cake.

Reading

Olympics with a difference

Have you ever seen wheelchair racing? No? Well, it's a very fast and exciting sport! The 'Paralympic Games' for disabled athletes are the world's second largest sports event after the Olympic Games. The 2012 Paralympic Games in London have 4,200 athletes from 150 countries doing 20 sports.

Shelly Woods (born 1986) *wheelchair racer*
Shelly Woods has used a wheelchair since she was eleven after she fell from a tree, as her legs are paralysed. Now she is one of the top British athletes. Shelly has won lots of medals, including a Silver and a Bronze at the 2008 Beijing Paralympics. She has also won a medal in the London Marathon. She trains six days a week but finds time to give talks in schools. The sport is very expensive. A racing chair costs £3,000 and only weighs about 5.5 kilograms!

Ben Rushgrove (born 1988) *runner*
Ben is deaf and has got cerebral palsy but he is a world-class runner. He has broken a world record and he won a silver medal in the Beijing Paralympics. Ben has also got a degree in sport from the University of Bath. Apart from training, he gives lots of talks in schools to inspire kids to do sport. In his spare time he likes watching films and TV, and hanging out with his friends.

Sarah Storey (born 1977) *cyclist*
Sarah Storey is an incredible athlete. She's got a deformed left hand, but she has won lots of gold, silver and bronze medals. She started as a swimmer when she was 14 years old, but changed to cycling in 2005. In 2008, she beat able-bodied cyclists in a 3,000-metre race. And in 2010, she raised money for Paralympic sports by doing a 1,600 kilometre, nine-day sponsored cycle ride across Britain.

1 Read the article and find:

1 four sports people: ath_lete_ ; ru_____ ; cy_____ ; sw_____
2 two parts of the body: le_____ ; ha_____
3 three metals: go_____ ; si_____ ; br_____
4 three places: Lo_____ ; Be_____ ; Br_____

2 Read the article again and complete the table.

	sport/s	disability	achievements and events	other activities / qualifications
Shelly Woods		paralysed legs	Beijing Olympics London Marathon	
Ben Rushgrove	runner			
Sarah Storey				sponsored cycle ride

Listening

3 ◉ **11** Listen to the sports commentaries and number the sports in the correct order. There are two sports not mentioned.

football ☐ basketball ☐ tennis ☐ running ☐ gymnastics ☐

4 ◉ **11** Write the sport for each description. Then listen again and check.

1 Davis passes the ball to Hart. *football*
2 Clarke is in the lead.
3 Taylor hits the ball high over the net.
4 There are only 200 metres to go.
5 He kicks the ball – and it's a goal!
6 It's 40-30. Match point to Taylor. Brodsky serves.

Writing

5 **Write a short essay about one of the following.**

My favourite sport
- some information about the sport and why you like it
- if you do it, say how well, who you play with, where you play, etc.
- if you watch it, describe the team you support, players, etc.

My favourite sports personality
- some information about the person: name, nationality, sport, etc.
- team or competitions the person is in, some of his/her achievements
- why you admire the person

> **Writing focus**
> If you use the internet, don't copy sentences. Instead make notes and write the information in your own words.

Your progress

Look at Student's Book Unit 3. Circle: ☹ = not very well ☺ = quite well 😎 = very well

I can ask and answer questions about experiences.	☹ ☺ 😎 p29
I can tell people about my life up to now, for example how long I have lived in my house.	☹ ☺ 😎 p33
I can read a leaflet about an award, understand the main points and guess the meaning of new words.	☹ ☺ 😎 p36
I can listen and understand people talking about their experiences.	☹ ☺ 😎 p37
I can write a paragraph summarising a plan for an adventure holiday.	☹ ☺ 😎 p37
I can make suggestions, check people's ideas, and agree and disagree.	☹ ☺ 😎 p110

Your project: achievements in my life

- Make notes about three things you are proud of. They can be big or small things!
  passing a piano exam   looking after my baby sister   winning a race
  painting a portrait of my mum   getting a good mark in English
  learning to swim
- Find things related to your achievements – photos, certificates.
- Say how you felt about the achievement.
- Give a mini-presentation to the class. Show them things related to your achievements.

I haven't bought her a present yet

1 Match the items on the list with the pictures.

a

b

c

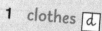
1 clothes ☑d
2 shoes ☐
3 phone cards ☐
4 make-up ☐
5 shampoo ☐
6 hair gel ☐
7 jewellery ☐
8 crisps ☐
9 magazines ☐
10 sweets ☐

d

e

f

g

h

i

j

2 Match the shops with the products.

1	a pharmacy	a	newspapers and magazines
2	a newsagent's	b	a keyboard and drums
3	a greengrocer's	c	medicine and soap
4	a butcher's	d	shirts and trousers
5	a music store	e	chocolate and sweets
6	a clothes shop	f	potatoes and peaches
7	a sports shop	g	tennis rackets and trainers
8	a sweet shop	h	chicken and sausages

Chat zone

12 Complete the conversations with the expressions. Then listen and check.

> ... you know.   Get a move on.   Hang on.

1 Luke   Debbie wants to come to the cinema with me this evening.

Matt   ....
You've already invited Tara!

2 Megan   Chicken again for dinner! Oh Mum, you know I hate it!

Mum   Sit down and eat, Megan. This isn't a restaurant, ...

3 Billy   ....
We'll be late.

Dean   It's only 7.30. The bus doesn't leave until 8.15!

Present perfect and *just*

1 Put the words in the correct order to make sentences.

1 great / bought / just / book / a / I've
   I've just bought a great book.

2 the / finished / we've / test / just
   ....

3 to / just / it's / rain / started
   ....

4 her / on / spent / all / just / clothes /
   she's / money
   ....

5 Brazil / they've / from / just / returned
   ....

6 email / he's / an / written / just
   ....

7 just / won / the / they've / basketball /
   championships
   ....

8 interesting / we've / just / an / seen /
   documentary
   ....

2 Complete the conversations with *just* and the present perfect form of the verbs.

> ask   send   have   land
> finish   start   ~~eat~~   buy

1 Would you like to have something to eat?
   No thanks. We 've just eaten lunch.

2 Are we late?
   No. The party ....

3 Why's Damian so red in the face?
   He .... the marathon.

4 Why's your hair wet, Elif?
   I .... a shower.

5 Does Zac know what time the film starts?
   Yes. I .... a text message.

6 Those trainers look really cool, Ethan.
   Thanks. I .... them at the
   shopping mall.

7 Why don't we ask Jenny to the party?
   I .... her!

8 What time does the plane land?
   It ....

Present perfect and *already/yet*

3 Write about what Jessica has already done and what she hasn't done yet.

1 clean her teeth
   Jessica's already cleaned her
   teeth.

2 recharge her mobile phone
   Jessica hasn't recharged her mobile
   phone yet.

3 have a shower
   ....
   ....

4 wrap her friend's birthday present
   ....
   ....

5 decide what to wear
   ....
   ....

6 dry her hair
   ....
   ....

7 put some CDs for the party in her bag
   ....
   ....

8 check her emails
   ....
   ....

4 **Match the beginnings and the ends of the sentences.**

1 I've just had dinner
2 He's just won the lottery
3 Mum's just seen my bedroom
4 My brother's just broken my mp3 player
5 I've just lost my wallet
6 It's just started to rain
7 I've just got the flu
8 They've just missed the bus

a so I'm staying in bed.
b so I haven't got any money.
c so she's not very happy.
d so they'll be late for school!
e so he's really happy.
f so I'm not hungry.
g so I'll take my umbrella.
h so I'll take his!

5 **Complete the sentences with *yet*, *just* or *already* and the correct form of the verbs in brackets.**

Debbie and Lyle ¹ *have just moved* (move) to a new city. They moved there last month. They ² .... (make) some new friends but they ³ .... (not see) all of the city ....

Lyle is a great drummer. He ⁴ .... (start) lessons at his new school but he ⁵ .... (not join) the school band ....

Debbie adores hip hop and she ⁶ .... (find) a great dance school.
They ⁷ .... (send) their old friends loads of photos and emails about their new life. Their mum and dad ⁸ .... (tell) them they can invite some old friends to stay next weekend – they're really happy. ☺

6 **Match the questions (1–8) with the answers (a–h).**

1 Have you finished that report, Erin? _h_
2 Can you tell me something about the new sports centre in town? ....
3 Has Maya sent those emails? ....
4 Has Miles found his watch yet? ....
5 Where's Tania? I can't find her anywhere. ....
6 Have you put some good music on your mp3 player? ....
7 Don't you think that's a great film? ....
8 Does Daniel know you like him? ....

a She's just gone out to get some bread.
b It's fantastic! I've already seen it three times at the cinema.
c He hasn't looked in the car yet.
d Yeah, she's just finished.
e I haven't learnt how to do it yet. Can you show me?
f I think so. I've just sent him a text message with a big heart on it!
g Of course. I've already been there four times this week.
h I've just finished the text but I haven't downloaded the photos yet.

1 Match the words with the pictures.

boy [2] middle-aged person ☐ girl ☐ baby ☐ toddler ☐ teenager ☐

1  2  3  4  5  6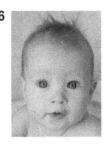

2 Look at the picture and count the people you can see.

In the picture there are …
.....three..... babies, ...
toddlers, ... children,
.... teenagers,
.... men, ...
women, ... middle-aged
people.

3 ⊙ 13 Complete the comments with the words. Then listen and check.

difficult   internet   home   get up   technology   love   ~~years~~   world

scarlett
Mum always says 'these are the best ¹ .....years..... of your life'. Well I don't think so!
All I hear at school and at ² .... is 'Do this', 'Do that', 'Don't wear this', 'Don't
think that'. Why can't I ³ .... late? Why do I have to do my homework? When
will somebody ⁴ .... me for who I am?

braveheart
People say being a teenager's ⁵ .... Well, I'm having a great time! I make
new friends every day on the ⁶ .... They write to me on my blog and we talk
about things that are really important to us. I know people from all over the
⁷ .... I can be anywhere at any time. ⁸ .... has changed everything!

Chat zone

⊙ 14 Complete the conversations with the expressions. Then listen and check.

tells me off   There's nothing wrong with …   having a laugh

1 **Zoe**   What's up, Maisie?
  Maisie Mum ....
       all the time. I can't do anything right!

2 **Rosie**   Mr Smith was angry with us in History
       but we were only
       ....
  Lauren No one has a sense of humour any
       more. ....
       having fun!

Indefinite pronouns

1 (Circle) the correct answers.

1 I've never seen (**anything**) / **nothing** so cool in my entire life!
2 They looked **somewhere** / **everywhere** but they couldn't find her.
3 My friend didn't give me **anything** / **nothing** for my birthday.
4 We didn't see **anybody** / **nobody** we knew at the disco.
5 Mum's taking me **somewhere** / **anywhere** really nice next weekend.
6 I'm so bored! **Anything** / **Nothing** interesting's happened recently.
7 There's **nobody** / **anybody** I like in that new reality TV show.
8 We should do **everything** / **something** possible to help Paula.

2 Complete the sentences with the words in the box.

> nothing   somebody (x2)   ~~anybody~~
> nobody   everywhere   something
> anywhere

1
I haven't sent ....._anybody_..... a text message. My mobile phone's broken.

2
We looked for you .... Where were you hanging out?

3
.... posted a great message on my blog. Was it you, Justin?

4
I didn't go .... yesterday. I was sick.

5
I've had .... to eat since this morning. I'm really hungry!

6
I'm going to tell you .... really important. Can you keep a secret?

7
We made a lot of noise and .... reported us to the headteacher!

8
.... told me the film started at 7 o'clock so I missed the beginning.

too / too much / too many / (not) enough   Ⓡ

3 (Circle) the correct answers.

1 There are **too much** / (**too many**) chairs.
2 We don't have **enough** / **too much** time to practise before the show.
3 Teenagers have **too many** / **too much** homework every night.
4 There aren't **too many** / **enough** people to organise the party.
5 There are **too much** / **too many** of us to go in one car!

4 Complete the conversation with *too, too much, too many* or *enough*.

Jade How was your summer course in Brighton, Erin?

Erin It was terrible! First of all, it was ¹ __too__ cold and it rained every day. Then there were ² _____ students in each class and the teachers gave us ³ _____ homework.

Jade Poor you! My course in Dublin was really cool but there wasn't ⁴ _____ time to visit all the interesting places in the city.

Erin We didn't visit any interesting places. I really wanted to go on the trip to London but the tickets cost ⁵ _____ .

Jade My college was great. What about yours?

Erin A disaster! There were ⁶ _____ rules and I had to go to bed ⁷ _____ early. There was never ⁸ _____ time to relax. It was worse than being at school. Next summer I'm staying at home!

Communication

15 Complete the conversation. Then listen and check.

much ~~help~~ I'll small got looking them size pair I'm

Shop assistant	Good morning. Can I ¹ __help__ you?
Customer	I'm ² _____ for some jeans.
Shop assistant	What ³ _____ are you?
Customer	⁴ _____ a small. Have you ⁵ _____ them in black?
Shop assistant	Here you are.
Customer	Can I try ⁶ _____ on?
Shop assistant	Of course you can.
Customer	They're a bit ⁷ _____ . Have you got a bigger ⁸ _____ ? How ⁹ _____ are they?
Shop assistant	They're £35.
Customer	¹⁰ _____ take them.

Reading

SHOPPING AROUND ✴✴✴✴✴✴✴✴✴✴✴✴✴✴✴✴✴✴✴✴✴✴✴✴✴

Middleton, Wisconsin, USA

We talked to American teenagers in a shopping mall about their shopping habits, and we discovered some interesting things! These teens are very careful with their money – they shop around and look at price and value for money. And they save their allowances and babysitting money for things they want.

Eddie, 14

My dad gives me an allowance of $30 a month. I love electronic things and computer games, but I don't buy them very often because they are too expensive. My friends and I swap games instead. I like going to the bowling alley with my friends or to the movies. It's better than shopping.

Jodie, 14

I like looking at clothes and jewelry. My friends and I go to stores that have our style. We often wait for a sale when the price goes down! But the best part for me is having an ice cream! Personally I don't buy things that are too fashionable – they don't last. When I'm with my mom, she buys things for me! That's cool.

Leo, 13

I don't hang out here. I usually come here with my parents. I hate shopping. I think it's boring and a waste of money. I don't need much at all. And I'm not interested in clothes. I think that we all buy too many things. We don't need most of them. That's why I think Buy Nothing Day is a good idea! I prefer recycling and making things, and helping the environment.

Caitlin, 15

I get $40 a month from my parents, and I do a bit of babysitting. But I'm saving up, so I can go on vacation to Mexico. I spend a bit on clothes and magazines but not that much. When I go shopping I often text my friends for advice. My best friend, Amy, advises me about fashion and color. She's very bossy!

---

1 Read the article and write the names of the teenagers. Who ...

    1 loves ice cream? ....

    2 does babysitting? ....

    3 gets an allowance? ....

    4 shops with their parents? ....

2 Match the beginnings and the ends of the sentences.

    1 Eddie likes electronic things

    2 Jodie and her friends

    3 Leo hates shopping

    4 Caitlin texts her friend

    5 Eddie prefers

    6 Caitlin doesn't spend her money

    a to get advice about what to buy.

    b because she is saving up for a vacation (holiday).

    c wait for the sales when the price is lower.

    d doing activities with friends.

    e because he thinks we all buy too much.

    f but they are too expensive.

Listening

3 🔘 **16** **Listen and match the names of the teenagers with the things they have bought.**

Andrew ☐ Samantha ☐ Jacob ☐ Megan ☐ Hannah ☐

1

2

3

4

5

4 🔘 **16** **Listen again. Why have they bought the things? Complete the answers.**

1 Andrew bought an mp3 player because ....

2 Samantha bought a book because ....

3 Jacob bought a magazine because ....

4 Megan bought some shoes because ....

5 Hannah bought a DVD because ....

Writing

5 **Using the article on page 34 as a model, write a paragraph about shopping.**

> **Writing focus**
>
> Use expressions from the article, e.g. *I like +
> -ing, I prefer ..., I think ...,
> Personally, I ..., I spend ...,
> When I go shopping, I ...* .

Your progress

Look at Student's Book Unit 4. Circle: 😕 = not very well 😊 = quite well 😎 = very well

I can talk about recent events, for example what I have done this month.	😕 😊 😎 p39
I can read personal views on a website and understand the general meaning.	😕 😊 😎 p43
I can give opinions and express my feelings about being a teen.	😕 😊 😎 p43
I can listen and understand the answers people give in a questionnaire.	😕 😊 😎 p47
I can write two paragraphs giving arguments for and against Buy Nothing Day.	😕 😊 😎 p47
I can go shopping and buy clothes, asking about sizes and prices.	😕 😊 😎 p111

Your project: our teen lives

- Write six questions for a survey about teen lives.
  How many texts do you send every day?
  How long do you spend doing your homework?
  Where do you hang out with your friends?
- Ask ten people your questions.
- Draw a graph of your results.
- Make a poster or a computer presentation. Find pictures on the internet
  or draw pictures to illustrate it.

1 Find the sixteen parts of the body in the word square.

arm

chest

ear

eye

fingers

foot

hair

hand

L	E	E	G	C	H	E	S	T	S
S	T	H	E	I	D	A	L	E	G
A	S	T	O	M	A	C	H	T	H
F	O	O	T	A	R	T	E	O	M
I	M	E	T	R	H	H	A	N	D
N	O	S	D	M	A	O	D	E	G
G	O	Y	W	A	I	S	T	C	P
E	Y	E	E	I	R	Q	C	K	X
R	F	A	E	R	A	N	O	S	E
S	E	R	M	O	U	T	H	E	R

head

leg

mouth

neck

nose

stomach

toes

waist

2 Complete the cartoons with these words.

cold	earache	cut	stomach ache	temperature	~~cough~~
sick	toothache	sore throat	~~headache~~	broken	

1

I've got a _headache_ and a _cough_ .

2

I've got a .... and a ....

3

I don't feel well. I think I've got a ....

4

I fell off my bike and I've got a .... arm. And I .... my head!

5

I've got .... and ....

6

I've eaten too much ice cream! I've got a .... and I feel ....

Chat zone

⊙ **17** Complete the conversations with the expressions. Then listen and check.

I'm feeling down   It's not your fault!
I'm so stressed out

1 **Alisha**   What's up, Ricky?
Ricky   ....
about the exams next week. I'll never be ready for them!

2 **Mum**   Cheer up, Olivia. What's the matter?
Olivia   ....
I've had an argument with my best friend.
Mum   Tell me all about it.
Olivia   She's annoyed because I went to Tania's birthday party.
Mum   But Tania didn't invite her.
....

Zero conditional

1 Put the words in the correct order to make sentences.

1 much / eat / you / if / too / feel / sick / you
If you eat too much, you feel sick.

2 hard / too / work / you / if / get / tired / you

3 competition / a / win / if / you / happy / you / feel

4 have / blog / a / if / you / can / friends / you / make

5 coat / a / if / wear / you / keep / you / warm / can

6 button / press / the / if / you / machine / the / starts

7 lot / of / you / if / exercise / do / a / can / fit / you / keep

8 do / if / homework / you / your / isn't / the / angry / teacher

First conditional

2 Match the beginnings and the ends of the sentences.

1 If we get an invite, [b]
2 If she finishes her homework, [ ]
3 If we go to Moscow, [ ]
4 If she comes to the party, [ ]
5 If we walk, [ ]
6 If they don't arrive soon, [ ]
7 If he stays up late, [ ]
8 If it's sunny tomorrow, [ ]

a she'll wear her new dress.
b we'll go to the party.
c he'll be tired.
d we'll be late.
e she'll come to the party.
f I'll cycle to school.
g they'll miss the beginning of the film.
h we'll go sightseeing.

3 (Circle) the correct answers.

The holiday of your dreams!

If you **¹ will spend /** (**spend**) your holiday with us, you **² have / will have** a holiday to remember! There's magic and mystery in this old Scottish castle. If you **³ walk / will walk** around the castle at night, you **⁴ meet / will meet** the ghost of a Scottish king. Are you brave? You **⁵ certainly find out / will certainly find out** if you **⁶ will decide / decide** to spend your holiday here because this castle is full of surprises.

There's lots for adults to do, too. If they **⁷ go / will go** for walks in the hills near the castle, they **⁸ see / will see** amazing views. There are some beautiful lakes and if they **⁹ go / will go** out in a boat with the local fishermen, they **¹⁰ will catch / catch** lots of fish for dinner.
So come to this castle in the Highlands of Scotland.

4 Read the questions and write responses using the first conditional.

1 Should I study for the test tomorrow?
If / not study for the test / not pass
If you don't study for the test, you won't pass.

2 Should we organise a school disco?
If / organise a school disco / have a great time

3 Should Luiza take the photos for the project with her new camera?
If / take the photos with her new camera / they / be fantastic

4 Should we practise for the concert after school tomorrow?
If / practise after school / I / not have time to do my homework

5 Should Nathan write about the concert on the class blog?
If / write about the concert on his blog / everyone / come

5 Complete the sentences for you.

1 If I don't do my homework,

2 If I go to a disco next Saturday,

3 If I don't go to bed before midnight,

4 If I watch too much TV,

5 If I work harder at school,

6 If I save my pocket money,

6 Complete the sentences with the correct form of the verbs in brackets.

1 Nathan Hi, Daniel. ......*Will*...... you
......*visit*...... (visit) me if I have to go to hospital?

Daniel Of course I .... We can listen to music and do crosswords.

2 Julia Mum, ... Dad .... (buy) me a present if he .... (go) to New York again for work?

Mum No, he .... No more presents until you get a better school report!

3 Ajay .... your parents .... (be) angry if you .... (not get) home before midnight?

Ethan Of course they ....!
They didn't let me go out for a week last time I was late.

4 Zoe If we .... (go) to a restaurant tonight, ... you .... (have) chicken?

Faye No, I .... I'll have a maxi burger.

7 Write questions. Then answer for you.

1 what / do / after school today?
What will you do after school today?
I'll visit my gran.

2 who / phone / this evening?

3 where / go / Saturday afternoon?

4 what programmes / watch on TV / tomorrow?

5 what time / go to bed / tonight?

1 Complete the descriptions of the people with the correct form of the verbs.

> tell jokes   be kind   get on with   damage things
> look after   help   have a laugh together   ~~tell lies~~

MY APARTMENT BLOCK

by Lola

These are some of the people who live in my apartment block. There are some amazing characters!

1

I travelled through the jungle on an elephant. Then I swam across the Pacific Ocean ...

My neighbour George sometimes _tells lies_. He just loves inventing stories!

2

Nick and Lucy often .... They are really good friends!

3

A man was walking along the road with a parrot on his head ...

My dad always .... He hears them at work and then tells them to us.

4

Tom lives on the second floor. He's only three years old. He often ....

5

Mrs Logan .... to young children. She often talks to them and gives them little gifts.

6

Eric .... his neighbours' plants when they are away. He's a nice guy.

7

Trish doesn't .... her brother. They often have arguments!

8

My mum sometimes .... me with my homework. She's very good at Maths!

2 Write about someone you know.

My brother is very funny. He often tells jokes.

Defining relative clauses

1 Circle the correct relative pronouns.

1 That's the trophy **which** / **who** we won in the tennis championship.

2 The White House is the place **who** / **where** the President of the United States lives.

3 The police caught the thief **which** / **who** stole my laptop.

4 I lost the book **who** / **which** you gave me for my birthday.

5 Mrs Smith's the teacher **which** / **who** helped me to pass the exam.

6 That's the mp3 player **who** / **which** Mum and Dad bought me.

7 Nelson Mandela's the man **who** / **which** fought apartheid in South Africa.

8 This is the town **which** / **where** I was born.

2 Complete the sentences with *who*, *which* or *where*.

1 Roald Dahl was the man ...._who_........ wrote *Charlie and the Chocolate Factory*.

2 The story is about a man .... gives his chocolate factory as a prize in a competition.

3 The chocolate factory is the place .... the adventure begins.

4 Charlie is the boy .... wins the prize.

5 In the factory, there is a room .... everything is made of chocolate.

6 One child eats a sweet .... makes her go purple.

7 The Oompa Loompas are the people .... work in the factory.

8 Tim Burton made a film .... stars Johnny Depp.

9 Johnny Depp is the actor .... plays the part of the factory owner.

3 Complete the email with *who*, *which* or *where*.

To: Anthony
From: Billy

Dear Anthony,
Today I'd like to tell you a bit about my school. It's in the small town ¹ ......_where_...... I was born. We start every morning at 8.15 am, and we finish at 3 pm. There are some teachers ² .... are really friendly and nice but the headteacher is very strict. I don't know anyone ³ .... isn't scared of him! The school's well organised. There are clubs ⁴ .... all the kids can meet in the afternoon and a canteen ⁵ .... serves really good food. The sports facilities are cool too. There's an Olympic-size swimming pool ⁶ .... we can also use at the weekend and two sports coaches ⁷ .... are really good at organising events with other schools in the area. What about your school? Is your headteacher scary, too?
Write soon,
Billy

4 Complete the sentences with *who*, *which* or *where*.

1 This is the neighbour ......_who_...... looks after my cat when I go away on holiday.

2 These are the sandwiches .... I brought to school today.

3 Istanbul is the city .... Ahmet's mum was born.

4 I can't find the DVDs .... my friends gave me for my birthday.

5 These are the photos .... I took in Peru.

6 Those are the boys .... swam in the sea yesterday.

7 That is the park .... I learnt to skateboard.

8 Those are the kids .... play volleyball with Mia.

5 Put the words in the correct order to make sentences.

1 is / have / place / the / a / you / shower / this / where
This is the place where you have a shower.

2 where / keep / is / place / you / clothes / this / the / your

3 cook / place / is / the / this / meals / you / the / where

4 sleep / place / to / you / is / go / where / this / the

5 put / the / where / the / is / car / place / this / you

6 find / is / place / a / this / armchairs / we / and / where / sofa / the

7 rice / find / place / the / and / where / coffee / is / you / pasta / this

8 relax / the / place / you / this / the / sunshine / in / is / where

6 Match the sentences from Exercise 5 with these places.

wardrobe ☐   bathroom 1   garden ☐
bedroom ☐   kitchen ☐   garage ☐
cupboard ☐   living room ☐

7 Rewrite the sentences with *who*, *which* or *where*.

1 This is the computer. I bought it last week.
This is the computer which I bought last week.

2 The Lumière is a cinema. We go there every weekend.
The Lumière is a cinema where we go every weekend.

3 I had a sandwich. It was awful!

4 Frank Lloyd Wright was the famous American architect. He designed the Guggenheim Museum in New York.

5 Where is the cake? It was in the fridge.

6 The National Gallery is a museum. You can see paintings by Leonardo da Vinci there.

Communication

◉ 18 Complete the conversations. Then listen and check.

| got | sport | I've | X-ray | sore | here's | problem | have | does | ~~seems~~ |

A

Doctor What ¹ *seems* to be the problem?

You I've got a ² .... throat.

Doctor Have you ³ .... a headache, too?

You Yes, I ⁴ ....

Doctor Let me examine you. ⁵ .... a prescription.

You Thank you, Doctor.

B

Doctor Good morning. What seems to be the ⁶ .... ?

You ⁷ .... got a pain in my ankle.

Doctor Did you do any ⁸ .... yesterday?

You Yes, I played football.

Doctor Let me examine you. ⁹ .... that hurt?

You Ouch! Yes, it does.

Doctor You should go to the hospital for an ¹⁰ ....

You OK. Thank you, Doctor.

Reading

IT'S YOUR WORLD

There are 194 countries in the world and each one is different, with its own history, traditions and culture. It is maybe surprising that 192 of these countries belong to the same global organisation – the United Nations or UN. So what is the UN and what does it do?

Fifty-one countries decided to create the UN on 24th October 1945, because they wanted to make a peaceful world after World War II. Since then the UN has grown – it aims to bring all the nations of the world together to stop wars and conflicts, improve people's lives, protect the environment and plan for the future. Did you know that 24th October is United Nations Day?

The UN has six official languages – Arabic, Mandarin Chinese, English, French, Russian and Spanish. The member countries meet once a year in September at a General Assembly. It is a moment when the world can talk about international problems and try to find solutions. Each country, large and small, rich or poor, has a single vote, although countries do not have to respect the decisions.

The United Nations international headquarters are in New York City – but the land the building is on is not American, it's international! It also has its own UN flag and postage stamp. Thousands of people work for UN organisations around the world – maybe you have heard of some of them. The Food and Agricultural Organisation (FAO) is based in Rome, and the United Nations Children's Fund (UNICEF) helps get food, water and medicine to children when there are disasters.

In 2000, the UN agreed to eight Millennium goals – stopping poverty and hunger; universal primary education; equality between men and women; saving babies' lives; saving mothers' lives; fighting disease; helping the environment; and helping countries develop.

Did you know that young people can take part too? There is a special youth UN called Model UN where school and university students take on the roles of UN diplomats and debate and vote on resolutions. They can do this in their schools or go to conferences around the world. Why not join in?

1 Read the article and find the numbers to complete the table.

The UN in numbers		number of votes per country	....
date the UN started	....	United Nations Day	....
number of members in 1945	....	number of official languages	....
number of members now	....	number of Millennium goals	....

2 Read the article again. Decide if the information is *right* or *wrong*, or if the article *doesn't say*.

1 There are 194 member countries in the UN. **a** right **b** wrong **c** doesn't say
2 The UN General Assembly is always in New York. **a** right **b** wrong **c** doesn't say
3 The UN headquarters are on American land in New York City. **a** right **b** wrong **c** doesn't say
4 The FAO and UNICEF are UN organisations. **a** right **b** wrong **c** doesn't say
5 Students can practise being diplomats in the Model UN. **a** right **b** wrong **c** doesn't say

Listening

3 ⊙ 19 **Listen and match the students with the problems.**

1 Louis ☐ 2 Skye ☐ 3 Owen ☐ 4 Martha ☐ 5 Jacob ☐

a lost friend's mp3 player **b** feels tired all the time **c** doesn't do homework at the weekend
d horrible boy in class **e** no close friends

4 ⊙ 20 **Match the students from Exercise 3 with the advice (there is one extra piece of advice).
Then listen and check your answers.**

a You should plan your free time. You can't do everything! ☐
b You should tell your friend the truth. ☐
c You should join some clubs and meet more people. ☐
d You should spend less time on your computer and do some exercise. ☐
e You shouldn't eat snacks between meals. ☐
f You should talk to your parents and your teacher. ☐

Writing

5 **Invent a problem and write to the *problem page*.
Then write Lizzie's answer to your problem.**

I AM LISTENING
Write to Lizzie with your problems!

Writing focus

If you like this activity, swap your problems with other students. Write your advice. Then choose the best answer.

Your progress

Look at Student's Book Unit 5. Circle: ☹ = not very well ☺ = quite well 😎 = very well

I can give and understand advice and respond to feelings.	☹ ☺ 😎	p49 p51
I can talk about my life, express my feelings, and say what I like and dislike.	☹ ☺ 😎	p53
I can describe myself and other people and explain preferences.	☹ ☺ 😎	p55
I can read an article about rights and understand the main points.	☹ ☺ 😎	p56
I can listen to stories about people's lives and understand the main points.	☹ ☺ 😎	p57
I can talk about my health with a doctor and communicate my feelings.	☹ ☺ 😎	p112

Your project: my favourite things

*   What are your five favourite possessions?
    my mascot   my mobile phone   a photo of my grandma
    my skateboard   my pet goldfish

*   Write a short explanation about each object. Say when you got it,
    where you keep it, why you like it, etc.

*   **Either**: take a photo of each possession and do a presentation to the class.

    Or: do a video presentation about your possessions at home. Show each one to
    the camera.

1 Read the clues and complete the crossword.

GREAT BIG TV CROSSWORD

Clues

1   where you hear about events in the world today: the ....

2   where you watch singers and dancers and vote: .... show.

4, 5   where you watch football, tennis, athletics, skiing, etc.

6, 3   where you watch a regular drama about a community or a street.

7   where you find out about historical events, science, etc.

8   where you watch animated characters, with music and sound effects.

9   where teams answer questions and win prizes: .... show.

10, 12   where you find out about animals around the world.

11   where comedians and actors perform sketches which make you laugh.

13   where a group of ordinary people or celebrities have to stay together, and each week you vote: .... show.

2 Complete the article with the words.

> ~~finalists~~ judges presenter winner audience contestants

Young Musician of the Year

Last night's final was very exciting. The three talented young
¹ _finalists_ gave absolutely fantastic performances. I loved the
violin concerto performed by 13-year-old Luke Fracassi, and 16-year-
old Lisa Hall's flute solo was brilliant. But 15-year-old Rosa Lin's
piano concerto was really amazing. The ² .... clapped for two
minutes! During the show the ³ .... interviewed each of the
⁴ .... They all felt happy after their performances. I wanted
them all to win! It was difficult for the panel of three ⁵ .... to
choose because the musicians were all so good. But they were most
positive about the pianist. So Rosa Lin was the ⁶ .... of this
year's competition. I wish her luck for the future. I'm sure she will be
successful.

Reported speech – statements

1 Complete the table with the pronouns and possessive adjectives.

her	them	his	~~she~~	they	their

direct speech	reported speech
I	he / ....she........
my	.... / her
me	him / ....
we	....
our	....
us	....

2 Complete the sentences with the correct personal pronouns.

1 'Chloe helps me with my homework,' said Billy.
Billy said Chloe helped ....him........ with his homework.

2 'Esra's running the marathon with me.'
Maisie said Esra was running the marathon with ....

3 'I love playing in the band!'
Mike said .... loved playing in the band.

4 'We hate wearing dresses!'
Anna and Millie said .... hated wearing dresses.

5 'Mrs Smith is teaching us photography.'
Gabriel said Mrs Smith was teaching .... photography.

6 'I'm going to buy Millie a new CD for her birthday.'
Rafael said .... was going to buy Millie a CD for her birthday.

3 (Circle) the correct answers.

1 I (told) / **said** him that I didn't want to go to the concert.

2 Maria **told** / **said** her mum was sick.

3 We **told** / **said** them we'd be late.

4 She **said** / **told** us she was in New York.

5 Mum **said** / **told** we had to be home early.

6 He **told** / **said** Melissa that she was clever.

4 Read the notes and complete the sentences.

She's got ...	She is ...
a house in the mountains ✗	married ✗
a bicycle ✓	from the local area ✗
a pet ✓	good at sport ✓
children ✗	good at using computers ✓
an mp3 player ✓	

1 Miss Scott said she ....had........ a pet.

2 She said she .... married.

3 She said she .... good at sport.

4 She told me she .... a house in the mountains.

5 Miss Scott told me she .... from the local area.

6 She said that she .... any children.

7 Miss Scott said she .... good at using computers.

8 She told me she .... an mp3 player.

5 Complete the sentences.

1 'I want to pass the exam,' said Luisa.
Luisa said she wanted to pass the exam.

2 'I love wearing jeans,' said Hannah.
Hannah said she ....

3 'I don't study Spanish,' said Thomas.
Thomas said he ....

4 'We're training for the tennis tournament,' said Kelly.
Kelly said they ....

5 'They're going to the disco on Saturday,' said Hiro.
Hiro said they ....

6 Report what Jasmine, Theo and Reuben are saying.

Jasmine

I'm living my dream.

I like being with the contestants.

I'm having a fantastic time.

I'm very nervous.

I'm going to give the best performance of my life.

I talk to my parents every day.

Theo

I get up at 5 o'clock every morning.

This is my last opportunity to become famous.

I'm working very hard.

Reuben

Jasmine
1 She said that she was living her dream.
2 ....
3 ....
Theo
1 ....
2 ....
3 ....
Reuben
1 ....
2 ....
3 ....

7 Imagine you are a finalist in *Pop Star*. Write what you are saying in the bubbles. Then complete the journalist's notes.

1 He/She said that
....
....

2 ....
....

3 ....
....

1 Match the jobs with the people on the set.

sound recordist ☐ camera operator ☐ make-up artist ☐ director ☐ scriptwriter ☐
producer ☐1 extras ☐ costume designer ☐ stunt artist ☐

2 Read what the people say and write the jobs.

❝ I do so many things. I read and help with the script. I talk to the producer and the designers. I work closely with the camera operators. But the most important thing is working with the actors. ❞

❝ It isn't a very exciting job. We just sit around a lot of the time. But it's fun to be on a film set. I never speak any words, but you can see me in lots of different films! ❞

❝ I usually start work very early in the morning, sometimes at 4 or 5 a.m. The actors are really tired, so I try not to talk too much. I enjoy making people look good. But I can make them look terrible, too! ❞

❝ It's a difficult job. Lots of people have opinions about my work and change what I write! But it's amazing when you hear people say your words for the first time. Then it's the best job in the world. ❞

❝ The worst thing about my job? Planes. And cars. You mustn't hear them in a film about Robin Hood! And mobile phones. They're the worst invention ever! ❞

1 *director*

2 ....

3 ....

4 ....

5 ....

Chat zone

◎ 21 **Complete the conversations with the expressions. Then listen and check.**

| check out   not really   I'm impressed! |

1 Tristan Hey, Martin! Was that your poem in the webzine this week?

Martin Yeah. I wrote it for the writing competition and I won!

Tristan ....

2 Mia You should .... that new reality show on TV tonight – it's really cool!

Emma That's a good idea. I love reality TV.

3 Beth Did you think the concert last night was good, Jake?

Jake No, ...
I enjoyed their last concert more.

Reported speech – modals

1 Complete the reported statements using modals.

1 'I have to go to work.'   Dad said he had to go to work.
2 'People will go to the Moon for their holidays.'   The journalist ....
3 'You must do exercises 1, 2 and 3.'   The teacher ....
4 'Nina can run really fast.'   The sports coach ....
5 'Our class won't win the competition.'   Rosa ....
6 'You mustn't run near the swimming pool.'   The lifeguard ....
7 'I can't find my mp3 player.'   Dylan ....
8 'I must remember Chrissie's birthday!'   Edward ....

2 Read the interview with Jamie and complete the article.

Journalist	Wow, Jamie, that was awesome! Congratulations.
Jamie	Thanks. It was fun!
Journalist	You've won the London Marathon so where do you go from here, Jamie?
Jamie	I'll spend every afternoon and evening training after school, of course. It won't be easy with final-year exams but I'll do my best.
Journalist	This is your last year at school. What are your plans?
Jamie	I'm going to America to study Sport Science at Harvard and I'm going to train with a really cool coach.
Journalist	Are you hoping to run for the Olympic team one day?
Jamie	Yes, I am. That's my dream. I'll have to work really hard but who knows? Maybe one day I'll surprise the world!
Journalist	Thanks, Jamie and all the best for the future.

Jamie Holmes was full of hopes for the future when I spoke to him at the finishing line earlier today.
He said he ¹ __would spend__ all his free time training for competitions. He told me it ² .... easy
with final-year exams but he ³ .... his best to keep on winning. When he finishes school this smart
young athlete said he ⁴ .... Sport Science in the USA and he
⁵ .... with one of their best coaches. He told me he
⁶ .... to compete in the Olympics one day. He said
he ⁷ .... train really hard but maybe one day he
⁸ .... the world.

We're sure he will!

Reported speech – *yes/no* questions

3 Complete the reported questions.

1 'Do you go to school on Saturday?'   He asked if I ....went.......... to school on Saturday.
2 'Are you studying for the exams?'   Mum asked if I .... studying for the exams.
3 'Is Sophie in the band?'   He asked if Sophie .... in the band.
4 'Are there any sweets in the bag?'   She asked if there .... any sweets in the bag.
5 'Is Ethan running in the marathon?'   The teacher asked if Ethan .... running in the marathon.

4   Read Matt's interview with Julian for the school survey. Then complete Julian's email to Megan.

Matt	Hi Julian. Can you answer some questions for the school survey?
Julian	Sure. Go ahead.
Matt	Are the lessons interesting?
Julian	Yeah, they are. Maths is my favourite, of course!
Matt	Are you happy about the exams next month?
Julian	Not really. I need to study more.
Matt	Thanks. Now, is the school day too long?
Julian	No, it isn't. It's fine.
Matt	Is the food in the canteen good?
Julian	The food's OK but we have to wait too long in the queue.
Matt	Last question. Is the school organising enough social activities?
Julian	Concerts, discos, parties, tournaments … there's no time to study!

To: Megan
From: Julian

Hi Megan,
The survey was quite good really. First he asked me if the lessons ¹ _were interesting_ and I said yes. Then he asked me if I ² .... about the exams next month and I said not really. Then he asked me if the school day ³ .... and I told him it ⁴ .... After that he asked me if the food in the canteen ⁵ .... and I said it ⁶ .... Finally he asked me if the school ⁷ .... enough social activities. I told him there ⁸ .... to study!
Love Julian

Communication

○ 22   **Complete the conversations. Then listen and check.**

leave	tell	give	where	called	spell	here	of course	~~take~~	this	OK	repeat

A

Tom	Hi. Can I speak to Bobby, please?
Leon	Bobby isn't here at the moment. Can I ¹ _take_ a message?
Tom	Yes, please. Can you tell him Tom ² .... ?
Leon	OK, I'll ³ .... him the message.

B

Naomi	Hi, can I speak to Damian, please?
Carrie	He isn't ⁴ .... Can I take a message?
Naomi	Yes, please. Can you ⁵ .... him I can't go to the cinema tomorrow?
Carrie	Could you ⁶ .... that, please?
Naomi	I can't go to the cinema tomorrow.
Carrie	⁷ .... , I'll give him the message.

C

Adam	Hello, ⁸ .... is Adam Wells.
Hannah	Can you ⁹ .... that, please?
Adam	W-E-L-L-S. Could I ¹⁰ .... a message for Lara?
Hannah	Yes, ¹¹ ....
Adam	I'll be at the bookshop at 10.
Hannah	¹² .... did you say?
Adam	At the bookshop.
Hannah	OK, I'll give her the message.

Reading

How much do you know about two of the coolest actors on the planet?

You know Robert Pattinson as an actor, but his first love was music. He has played the piano since he was three and the guitar since he was five! He composes music, and co-wrote and sang two songs for the film *Twilight*. His sister Lizzy is musical, too – she is a singer and songwriter. Robert became interested in theatre when he was 15, but he didn't act at first – he helped backstage! His first film role was in 2003 as Cedric Diggory in a Harry Potter film. But Robert really became famous with the role of Edward Cullen in the Twilight films. Fans all over the world adore him.

Robert has other talents – he was not only an actor in the 2010 romantic film *Remember me*, he was also a producer.

Surprisingly, Robert is not keen on sport, but he learnt to scuba dive for the Harry Potter film. He lives in Los Angeles for part of the year and supports a charity for homeless people there.

Name Robert Pattinson
Born 13 May 1986, London
Height 1m 85

Hilary Duff comes from a talented family. Her mother is a film producer and her sister Haylie is an actor and singer-songwriter. Hilary started in the acting world very early. She and Haylie performed in a professional ballet company when she was six. Hilary took acting lessons too, and appeared in TV adverts and performed in theatres.

In 2001, Hilary starred in the TV series *Lizzie McGuire*, which two million teenagers watched every week. Since then she has starred in the film *Cadet Kelly*. For many of the films she has also been a producer. Hilary is also famous for her music and has sold millions of records. She recorded her first album when she was only 15 and she sometimes writes songs. And that's not all! In 2004, she launched a fashion company called *Stuff by Hilary Duff*, and she has her own best-selling perfume. Now she has written *Elixir*, a novel for young adults! Hilary also works for animal and children's charities and she donated $250,000 to the victims of Hurricane Katrina.

Name Hilary Duff
Born 28 September
1987, Houston
Height 1m 57

---

1   **Read the article. Are the sentences true (*T*) or false (*F*)?**

   1   Robert Pattinson plays the piano and the guitar. ....T........

   2   He starred as Cedric Diggory in the Twilight films. ....

   3   He lives in Los Angeles all the time. ....

   4   Hilary Duff acted in the theatre when she was six. ....

   5   *Cadet Kelly* was one of her films. ....

   6   She is also a singer and she has written a novel. ....

2   **Read the article again. Tick (✓) the things Robert and Hilary have in common.**

   have been film producers ☐   have written a novel ☐   write some of their own songs ☐

   have sung in films ☐   were born in the USA ☐   have a sister who sings and writes songs ☐

   performed at the age of six ☐   support charities ☐   own a fashion business ☐

Listening

3 🔘 **23** Listen and match the actors with the information.

1 Penélope Cruz   **2** Orlando Bloom   **3** Kristen Stewart   **4** Keira Knightley   **5** Johnny Depp

a has an Australian mother ☐   **b** supports Manchester United ☐   **c** is scared of clowns ☐

d can speak four languages ☐   **e** middle name is Jaymes ☐   **f** has had a lot of accidents ☐

g owns a clothes shop ☐ 1   **h** supports West Ham United ☐   **i** has dyslexia ☐

j co-owns a Hollywood restaurant ☐

Writing

4   **Write a short biography about your favourite actor. Research on the internet and make notes.**

where born .... ; physical appearance .... ;
family and childhood .... ; films .... ;
other talents or skills .... ; trivia ....

Writing focus

A mind map is useful for this sort of writing activity.

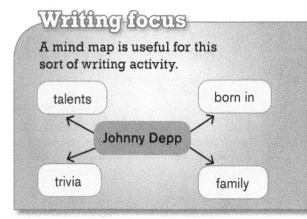

talents — born in — Johnny Depp — trivia — family

Your progress

Look at Student's Book Unit 6. Circle: 🙂 = not very well 😊 = quite well 😎 = very well

I can read and understand the facts and information in a TV review.	🙂 😊 😎	p59
I can talk about a film I like, giving key information about it.	🙂 😊 😎	p63
I can read an article about making films and understand the main ideas.	🙂 😊 😎	p66
I can listen to people talking about their jobs and catch the main points.	🙂 😊 😎	p67
I can talk about my education and future career.	🙂 😊 😎	p67
I can leave and take telephone messages, writing them down for other people.	🙂 😊 😎	p113

Your project: my favourite film

- Make a list of your favourite films and films you don't like.
- Choose one of the films and make notes about these things:
  the title   the year   the director   the type of film   the story
  the main characters   the actors   the special effects
  the music   the costumes   why you like it
- Write a review of the film. Give it a star rating: - 1 = bad   5 = good.
- Do a class presentation about your film.

1 Complete the table with the type of criminal.

CRIME	ACTION	CRIMINAL
mugging	to mug (someone)	mugger
vandalism	to vandalise (a place) to damage (a place)	
burglary	to break into (a building)	
theft	to steal (something from someone)	
shoplifting	to shoplift to steal (from a shop)	
pickpocketing	to pickpocket / to steal	

CRIME SCENE DO NOT CROSS *CRIME SCENE DO NOT CROSS*

2 Complete the stories with the correct words from Exercise 1.

| Home | News and views | Sport Competitions | | | |

Got a story? Call the Newsdesk or send us an email

1 Car theft
........Thieves........ broke the windows of six parked cars in Leafield Street last night and stole car radios and other items including a laptop.

2 Be careful!
Watch your bags and possessions when you are out and about this weekend. There is a gang of .... in the city centre.

3 Garden shock
Contestants in the Barton Garden Competition woke up to a terrible surprise yesterday. Damaged flower beds, broken plants and graffiti. Gardener Terry Hall said, 'We must stop this .... !'

4 Student victims
A .... broke into a student house in Cambridge last night and stole two games consoles and three laptops.

5 Mugged for a mobile
A teenage boy was the victim of a .... at 10 p.m. last night. He was walking home when the .... stopped him and took his mobile phone.

6 Millionaire's son arrested
The 17-year-old son of multi-millionaire Bill Sykes was arrested yesterday for .... Police found several items in his rucksack, stolen from stores in the new shopping centre in the city.

Second conditional statements

1 **Write sentences using the second conditional.**

1 If / be / in Cairo / see / the Pyramids
If I were in Cairo, I would see the Pyramids.

2 If / visit / Egypt / go / on a boat trip down the Nile

....

....

3 If / can / choose my perfect holiday / do something adventurous

....

....

4 If / climb / a mountain / leave / a flag on the top

....

....

5 If / spend / my summer on a tropical island / be / the happiest person in the world

....

....

6 If / not be / too tired / dance / every night on the beach

....

....

7 If / have / more money / fly / to New York

....

....

8 If / not be / too scared / take / photos from the top of the Empire State Building

....

....

2 **Match the beginnings and the ends of the sentences.**

1 I'd buy a Ferrari `b`
2 I'd argue with my best friend ☐
3 I wouldn't be happy at school ☐
4 I'd go to bed early ☐
5 I'd train every day ☐
6 I'd be really excited ☐

a if I won a competition.
b if I could drive.
c if I was on the school football team.
d if I had a test in class tomorrow.
e if she didn't invite me to her party.
f if I didn't like my teacher.

3 **Complete the sentences for you.**

1 If I had a million dollars, ...
I'd take my family on an amazing holiday.

2 If I heard a strange noise in the middle of the night, ...

....

....

3 If I saw a huge spider in the bathroom, ...

....

....

4 I would feel very happy if ...

....

....

5 If I lived in China, ...

....

....

6 If I were really late for school, ...

....

....

7 My parents would be annoyed with me if ...

....

....

8 If I couldn't find my mobile phone, ...

....

....

....

Second conditional questions and short answers

4 Write questions and positive (✓) or negative (✗) short answers.

1 you have fun / you go to the Olympic Games (✓)
   Would you have fun if you went to the Olympic Games? Yes, I would.

2 Ellen feel better / she take some medicine (✓)

3 Jamie win the race / he not train every day (✗)

4 the garden be prettier / we plant more flowers (✓)

5 Madison look nicer / she cut her hair (✗)

6 you be tired / you not go to bed before midnight (✓)

7 we help the environment / we recycle paper, glass and plastic (✓)

8 Juan be angry / I borrow his pen (✗)

5 Write questions using the second conditional.

1 you invent an excuse / you forget to do / your homework?
   Would you invent an excuse if you forgot to do your homework?

2 you clean his car every day / your dad / pay you well?

3 you wear the same clothes as your friend / you go out together?

4 you go to a party / your mum not want / you to go?

5 you be honest / your friend's new haircut be really awful?

6 you tell the truth / you not like the present your best friend / give you?

7 you help a friend / he cannot answer the questions during a test?

6 Answer the questions from Exercise 5 for you.

1 Match the headings with the students' opinions.

> School for everyone   Saving animals   World peace   The environment
> A better town or city   ~~Helping poor people~~

What is most important to you?
We asked our readers to send us their thoughts. And here are your answers.

1   Helping poor people

People in rich countries should help other countries. We have so many things and we can share them.   Tyler, *New York*

2 ....

We should think local – if we all sort out the problems near our home then the world will be a better place.   Alexis, *El Paso*

3 ....

Of course I worry about lions, elephants, tigers. But we have to think about our animals nearer to home. We've got beautiful birds, reptiles and mammals which need our help.   Brianna, *Sacramento*

4 ....

I hate war. It destroys people's lives and their countries. It kills people and they live in fear.   Eric, *Washington DC*

5 ....

I worry about pollution and global warming. We all have to work together to protect our world. We can all help by recycling and cleaning up our local areas.   Zachary, *Seattle*

6 ....

It's important for all children to get an education. They will have a better future if they have qualifications.   Lauren, *Memphis*

2 Complete the spidergrams. Use the words on this page and other words you know.

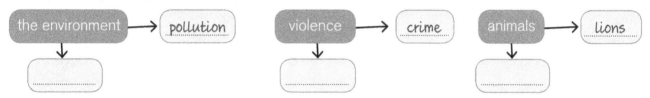

the environment → pollution → ⬇ [ ]

violence → crime → ⬇ [ ]

animals → lions → ⬇ [ ]

Chat zone

⊙ 24 Complete the conversations with the expressions. Then listen and check.

> But seriously   I think it's rubbish!   Get a life!   loads of

1 Naomi   What did you do at the weekend, Henry?

Henry   Not much. I watched TV on Saturday and Sunday evening.

Naomi   .... Why do you waste your time watching TV?

2 Bethany   Mrs Jones gave us .... homework!

Justin   I know. I'll never finish it all.

3 Rosie   Are you watching that new reality show on TV this afternoon?

Jessica   No! .... How can you watch that stuff?

Rosie   Oh, I think it's great.

Jessica   ...., do you really like it? It's so boring!

Second conditional *wh*-questions

1 Complete the questions with the correct form of the verbs in brackets. Then answer the questions for you.

1 Where would you live if you ....*were*........ (be) a famous film star?

....

2 What would you take with you if you .... (go) to the Moon?

....

3 Who would you talk to if you .... (feel) sad?

....

4 Who would you go with if you .... (win) a holiday for two people?

....

5 Where would you go if you .... (can) visit any country?

....

6 What would you buy if you .... (have) loads of money?

....

2 Write questions.

1 What / the teacher do / see / you sending a text message in class?
What would the teacher do if she saw you sending a text message in class?

2 What / your mum do / your room / be / really messy?

3 What / your best friend do / you / tell someone all her secrets?

4 What / you do / the teacher / choose / you to be the star of the school play?

5 What / happen / you / not wash for a week?

6 What / you do / someone / steal your mp3 player?

3 Match the answers with the questions from Exercise 2.

a She wouldn't be my best friend any more! ☐ 3

b She'd send me out of the class. ☐

c Mum would send me to have a shower immediately! ☐

d I'd die of embarrassment! ☐

e I'd tell the teacher. ☐

f She'd tell me to tidy it. ☐

4 Complete the questions with the correct form of the verbs in brackets. Then answer the questions for you.

1 What <u>would you do</u> (do) if your uncle <u>gave</u> (give) you €100?

2 What .... you .... (see) if you .... (go) to the cinema tonight?

3 What gadget .... you .... (buy) if you .... (get) some money for your birthday?

4 What sport .... you .... (do) if you .... (be) in the Olympic team?

5 What .... you .... (do) if the dog .... (eat) your homework?

6 How .... you .... (celebrate) if your favourite team .... (win) the World Cup?

5 Complete the sentences for you. Use your imagination!

1 If I were an animal, I'd be *a horse because they are intelligent and beautiful.*

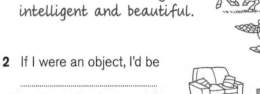

2 If I were an object, I'd be

....

....

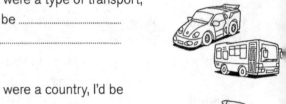

3 If I were a type of transport, I'd be ....

....

4 If I were a country, I'd be

....

....

5 If I were a type of music, I'd be ....

....

6 If I were a musical instrument, I'd be ....

....

7 If I were a fruit, I'd be

....

....

8 If I were a famous person in history, I'd be ....

a little / a few

6 **Write the words in the correct column.**

> people ~~water~~ CD ~~bottle~~ English day
> car decoration traffic money Euro
> milk concert sugar homework bread

Countable	Uncountable
bottle	water
....	....
....	....
....	....
....	....
....	....
....	....

7 **Circle the correct answers.**

1 I've only been to **a little /** **a few** concerts.

2 Add **a little / a few** decorations and your card will be great!

3 Ben speaks **a little / a few** German but his English is better.

4 Can I have **a little / a few** more sugar in my tea, please?

5 If you spent **a little / a few** more time studying, you'd pass the exam.

6 **A little / A few** people think using computers is bad for kids.

7 Henry got **a little / a few** money for his birthday.

8 I've only got **a little / a few** CDs – I prefer using my mp3 player.

Communication

25 **Complete the conversations. Then listen and check.**

> were a problem idea ~~don't~~ try the trouble sure should

A

Ryan I've got **1**.................................... with yesterday's ICT homework.

Megan If I **2**.................................... you, I'd ask Simon.

Ryan I'm not **3**.................................... that's a good idea. Simon wasn't at school yesterday!

Megan Why don't you ask the ICT teacher?

Ryan Thanks. I'll **4**.................................... that.

B

Carrie I'm not feeling well.

Brittany Why **5** *don't* you go home?

Carrie **6**.................................... is there's a Geography test next lesson.

Brittany I think you **7**.................................... talk to the teacher.

Carrie That's a good **8**.................................... .

Reading

1 Read the article and write the headings above the paragraphs.

Make a teen space   Help at an animal shelter   Plant a tree
Have a street party   Visit elderly people   ~~Run a Book Drive~~

Make a Difference Day

On the fourth Saturday in October millions of people in the USA and the UK make a difference to their communities and raise money for charity. Make a Difference Day is easy to take part in and it's fun – there are lots of projects to do with your friends or family. Just take a look at some of the things going on in Ohio, USA.

A .... Run a Book Drive

Many families have old books they've read. These books can help children in poor families to learn to read. Collect books around your area and sort them out. See the kids' faces when you give them out!

B ....

Be a 'pal' to elderly people by helping them out in their homes. Join us on Saturday. You can tidy their garden, make a meal or help them sort out their attic. Or why not teach them computer skills, play chess or just sit and have a chat?

C ....

Your local play areas need trees. Join a local group to plant trees and make an eco-wood. It's fun and it's green. And you will make a difference for generations to come!

D ....

Celebrate your area and meet your neighbours with a street party. Have a barbecue and play silly games! Why not arrange a karaoke event? You can collect money for a local charity at the same time.

E ....

Do you love animals? Then you can help at your local animal shelter. Clean the cages or prepare the food, take the dogs for a walk or maybe just help in the office. And don't forget to give the animals a hug!

F ....

Join us in transforming an empty building into a youth centre. Clean up rooms, paint walls, set up computers and create a games room. Or you could build a tree house to hang out in. Make a difference for teens!

2 Read the article again. Where can you ...

1 clean or wash things? E F
2 tidy, or sort out things? ....
3 plant things? ....
4 play games? ....
5 cook? ....
6 paint things? ....

3 Match the words (1–5) with the definitions (a–e).

1 set up
2 clean up
3 sort out
4 hang out
5 take part in

a clean and tidy a place
b join an activity or event
c organise an event or an activity
d see your friends and be with them
e put things in order

Listening

4 🔘 **26** Listen to the conversation between Jenny and Nick and complete the leaflet.

Make a Difference Day

Join the Big Wildlife Park Clean-up
Collect rubbish, build a pond, put up bird boxes,
paint benches and plant trees.

Date	1..
Time	Begins 2..
	Ends 3..
To book a place, contact	4..
Telephone number	5..
Last date to book	6..
Must bring with you	7..

Writing

5 Choose an activity from the article on page 58.
Imagine you took part in *Make a Difference Day*.
Write about the day. First make some notes:

- what you did, when and where
- who you did it with
- something funny or interesting that happened
- what you thought of the day

Writing focus

Making notes is a useful stage when you write. It gives you time to think of ideas, organise them and think of the best words.

Your progress

Look at Student's Book Unit 7. Circle: 😕 = not very well 🙂 = quite well 😎 = very well

I can talk about imaginary situations and keep a conversation going.	😕 🙂 😎	p69 p73
I can read a webzine about changing the world and contribute my own opinion.	😕 🙂 😎	p73
I can read and understand an article about School Councils.	😕 🙂 😎	p76
I can listen and understand the main points of people's opinions and concerns.	😕 🙂 😎	p77
I can write about my opinion, giving reasons for and against a statement.	😕 🙂 😎	p77
I can give and accept advice and express doubt about an idea.	😕 🙂 😎	p114

Your project: what I care about

- Think about two issues that you really care about. Here are some ideas:
  endangered animals   the environment   poverty   my neighbourhood   music
  a cure for serious illnesses   my football team   healthy eating   world peace
- Write a paragraph about each issue. Include:
  what issue it is
  why you care
  what you or other people can do
- Find photos on the internet or draw pictures to illustrate each one and make a poster.

1 Find the past participles of the verbs in the word square.

break
build
buy
do
drink
drive
eat
find
give
grow
make
put

T	A	K	D	B	U	Y	S	L	E	P	T	G	A
W	C	G	R	O	W	N	M	A	T	W	O	I	G
R	N	S	B	W	B	X	T	A	K	E	N	V	F
O	G	O	U	P	U	T	D	B	O	U	G	E	E
M	A	W	I	V	I	E	R	I	D	D	E	N	O
B	V	M	L	L	R	U	W	O	N	S	F	E	
O	W	R	I	T	T	E	N	F	N	R	P	O	R
U	D	R	O	Y	T	A	K	E	E	M	E	U	O
G	O	R	E	O	U	D	I	S	Q	A	B	N	D
H	E	P	K	U	S	T	D	R	A	D	R	W	E
T	S	U	N	G	E	A	T	E	N	E	O	O	H
G	R	U	W	H	N	F	L	E	S	X	K	R	S
S	P	E	N	T	T	A	S	P	O	K	E	N	O
O	D	R	I	V	E	N	B	Z	L	J	N	I	K
L	S	E	N	J	F	O	U	N	D	A	S	A	N

read
ride
sell
send
sing
sleep
speak
spend
take
wear
win
write

2 Complete the sentences with the past participles of the verbs.

wear   make   drive   drink   ~~grow~~   send   ride   speak

Where in the world…?

1 Bananas are ......_grown_...... in Brazil.

2 A lot of coffee is .... in France.

3 In the UK and Ireland cars are .... on the left.

4 More text messages are .... in China than any other country.

5 Camels are .... in Egypt and the Middle East.

6 Both English and French are .... in Canada.

7 Helmets are .... by all cyclists in New Zealand.

8 Suzuki cars are .... in factories in Japan.

Chat zone

◎ **27** Complete the conversations with the expressions. Then listen and check.

actually   sort of   It's a bit like

1 **William** Is it fun having your own blog, Harry?

Harry Yeah, it's really cool.

....

having a second life with different friends and different things to do!

2 **Mum** You're always sitting in front of that computer, Trisha!

Trisha That's so unfair, Mum! Most of the time I .... use it to do my homework.

3 **Livia** Hi, Tania. We had a great English class today. We wrote a class blog!

Tania What exactly is a class blog?

Livia Well, it's a type of class diary. But .... more public because we put it on the internet!

Present passive positive and negative

1 Complete the sentences with the correct form of the passive.

1 Maths ___is studied___ (study) in most schools in Europe.

2 Letters _____ (not write) very often today.

3 Rice _____ (eat) a lot in China.

4 Italian _____ (not speak) in many countries.

5 Lots of text messages _____ (send) every day.

6 Comments _____ (post) on blogs.

7 Latin _____ (not teach) in many schools in England.

8 Interesting websites _____ (find) on the internet.

2 Change the active sentences into passive ones.

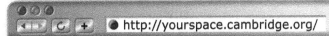
http://yourspace.cambridge.org/

ABOUT OUR SCHOOL

1 The Music teacher trains the orchestra after school.
The orchestra is trained after school by the Music teacher.

2 My class collects money for charity every month.

3 The canteen recycles all our organic waste.

4 Our teacher doesn't tolerate bad behaviour in class.

5 The Parents' Association raises funds for school trips.

6 The English teacher shows a film in English every Friday evening.

7 Each class chooses a student to be class representative.

8 Many parents give the students sandwiches for lunch.

3 Complete the text with the passive form of the verbs in brackets.

How a book is made

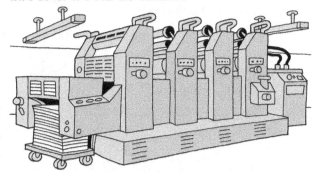

First the author writes a story and sends it to a publisher. The story ¹ ___is read___ (read) by an editor, and if the editor likes it, a contract ² _____ (send) to the author. Then the story ³ _____ (prepare) carefully by a book editor. The book ⁴ _____ (design) by a designer on a computer, and sometimes an illustrator ⁵ _____ (commission) for the cover picture. After a lot of work, the book is ready and a disk ⁶ _____ (send) to the printer. Page proofs ⁷ _____ (produce) by the printer on big machines. These proofs ⁸ _____ (check) for mistakes by an editor. After that, the pages ⁹ _____ (print), then they ¹⁰ _____ (cut) and put together to make the books. Finally the books ¹¹ _____ (deliver) to bookshops. If the author is lucky, lots of the books ¹² _____ (sell)!

Present passive questions and short answers

4 Write questions and positive (✓) or negative (✗) short answers.

1 your teeth / check / every three years? (✗)
Are your teeth checked every three years?
No, they aren't.

2 pizza / cook / cool oven? (✗)

....

....

3 the Queen's picture / print / on a British stamp? (✓)

....

....

4 an antivirus / use / to protect a computer? (✓)

....

....

5 pasta / make from / flour and milk? (✗)

....

....

6 Toyota cars / produce / Japan? (✓)

....

....

7 tea / drink / only in the UK? (✗)

....

....

8 fish and chips / eat / England? (✓)

....

....

9 rugby / play / with a round ball? (✗)

....

....

10 tigers / find / in India? (✓)

....

....

11 hotel rooms / clean / every day? (✓)

....

....

12 that song / sing / at the stadium? (✗)

....

....

5 🔘 **28** Complete the interview with the correct form of the verbs in brackets or short answer. Then listen and check.

The secrets of film making
by Clare Fox

This week we interview one of today's best young film directors – Jake Russo. And he tells us all about the world of film-making.

Clare Jake, how ¹ *is* a film *made* (make)?

Jake Well, the first thing to say is – a film ² .... (not make) by just one person. Because I'm a successful director, people often think that I do everything. And that isn't true!

Clare How ³ .... the story .... (choose)?

Jake Often the film ⁴ .... (not choose) by the director. It is chosen by the producers. Remember, the producers have all the money! So they're very important.

Clare So what happens next? ⁵ .... the script .... (write)?

Jake No, it ⁶ .... First the scenes are planned very carefully. We take a long time over this. It's probably the most important stage.

Clare When ⁷ .... the actors .... (choose)?

Jake The actors are usually chosen when our plan, or the script, is finished.

Clare Who ⁸ .... the actors .... (select) by?

Jake They're selected by me. But not only by me, of course. The producers are often there, and so are my assistants.

Clare ⁹ .... all the scenes .... (film) on location?

Jake No, they ¹⁰ .... Some scenes are filmed in a studio.

Clare Does a film take a long time to make?

Jake Yes, it does. It ¹¹ .... (not finish) in a couple of weeks! It can take a year, or even longer!

Clare When ¹² .... the music .... (add)?

Jake The music and the sound are added at the end, after the film is edited. Then the film is printed. And finally it is distributed to cinemas all around the world. And hopefully, it becomes a great success!

1 Unscramble the letters and label the punctuation marks.

1 SONTEUIQ KRAM   2 EPCSEH SRAKM   3 LOONC

4 NHPEYH   5 SHAD   6 LIAPATC TRETEL   7 TESHORAPOP

8 MOCAM   9 LULF POTS   10 TAILCANXEMO RAKM

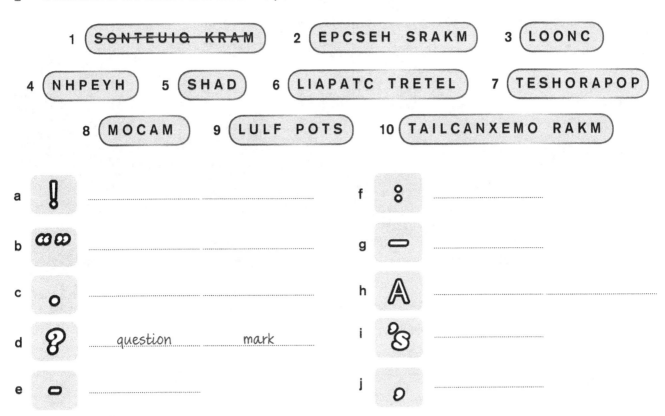

a ....

f ....

b ....

g ....

c ....

h ....

d question   mark

i ....

e ....

j ....

2 Rewrite the email with the correct punctuation marks.
Add capital letters where necessary.

> **MESSAGE...**
>
> hi mark
>
> how are you [question mark] i had a cool surprise today [full stop] a package was delivered this morning [dash] with my birthday present in it [exclamation mark]
>
> do you remember i had a three [hyphen] year [hyphen] old mobile [question mark] well [comma] now i [apostrophe] ve got a new one [exclamation mark] it [apostrophe] s got loads of features [colon] a camera [comma] internet [comma] games [comma] maps and music [full stop] my sister said [comma] [speech marks] it [apostrophe] s the best phone ever [exclamation mark] [speech marks] so send me a text soon [exclamation mark]
>
> george

> **MESSAGE...**
>
> ....
> ....
> ....
> ....
> ....
> ....

Past passive

1 Complete the text with the past passive form of the verbs in brackets.

The Empire State Building **1** ..was..designed.. (design) by William F. Lamb in 1929. Construction **2** .... (start) on 17th March, 1930 by 3,400 workers. A lot of immigrants from Europe **3** .... (involve) in the project and five workers **4** .... (kill) before it **5** .... (complete) in 1931.

The Empire State Building **6** .... (build) with 102 floors, 6,500 windows and 73 lifts.

It **7** .... (know) as the world's tallest building until work on the World Trade Center's North Tower **8** .... (finish) in 1972. After the World Trade Center **9** .... (destroy) in 2001, the Empire State Building became the tallest building in New York City once again. In 2007, 1,000 businesses **10** .... (locate) inside the building.

The Empire State Building

2 Write questions using the past passive.

Famous Firsts!

① When / the first plane / fly?

② Where / the first game of basketball / play?

③ When / the first telescope / use?

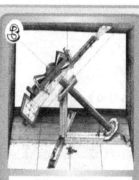

④ Who / the first catapults / design / by?

⑤ Who / the first sandwich / eat / by?

⑥ Where / the first hot dogs / sell?

1 When was the first plane flown?
2 .... ?
3 .... ?
4 .... ?
5 .... ?
6 .... ?

3 Circle the correct answers to the questions from Exercise 2.

1 The first plane was flown in ... **a** 1890. **b** 1900. **c** 1903.
2 The first game of basketball was played in ... **a** Australia. **b** America. **c** Canada.
3 The first telescope was used by Galileo in ... **a** 1509. **b** 1609. **c** 1709.
4 The first catapults were designed by the ... **a** Etruscans. **b** ancient Romans. **c** ancient Greeks.
5 The first sandwich was eaten by ... **a** an actor. **b** a soldier. **c** a king.
6 The first hot dogs were sold in ... **a** London. **b** Paris. **c** New York.

4 Complete the questions with the correct form of the verbs in brackets. Then write positive (✓) or negative (✗) short answers.

1 **Mum** <u>Were you chosen</u> (you / choose) to play in the school orchestra this year?

Jade (✗) <u>No, I wasn't.</u> The teacher says I have to wait until next year!

2 **Anna** .... (Victor / ask) to take part in the inter-school art contest?

Beth (✓) .... His work's so cool, I'm sure we'll win!

3 **Billy** .... (enough money / raise) in the town centre on Saturday morning?

Jacob (✓) .... We've got enough to buy a new computer for the writing club.

4 **Daniel** .... (the party invitations / send) last week?

Luke (✓) .... I hope everyone will come!

5 Write questions. Then answer the questions for you.

1 your school / build / in the last century? Was your school built in the last century?

2 your mobile phone / make / in Japan?
....
....

3 your family's car / manufacture / in Italy?
....

4 your schoolbag / buy / in a shopping centre?
....

5 your trainers / produce / in China?
....

6 your class / give / a lot of homework yesterday?
....

7 your school / award / any prizes last year?
....
....

Communication

○ 29 Complete the conversations. Then listen and check.

why ~~what's~~ feel look up because alright terrifying

A

Noah ¹ <u>What's</u> wrong? You look scared.

Lauren I am! I've just finished this book. It was ² .... !

B

Ben What's ³ .... ?

Adrian I feel really bored.

Ben Why do you feel bored?

Adrian ⁴ .... it's raining and I want to go swimming.

C

Luke You ⁵ .... happy.

Kay I am! I've won a poetry competition!

D

Cassie Are you ⁶ .... ?

Lily Not really. I ⁷ .... very nervous.

Cassie ⁸ .... do you feel nervous?

Lily Because I've got an exam tomorrow and I haven't done any work!

Reading

1 Match the pictures with the inventions in the text.

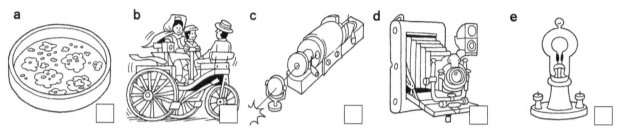

a   b   c   d   e

FIVE inventions that made the modern world

1 Camera   We take photos on our phones and share them with our friends in seconds. But when the first camera was invented in 1827, it took eight hours to develop the photos! In 1888, the American George Eastman invented the 'Kodak photographic machine' which was smaller and had flexible film. Suddenly ordinary people could take photos. Early photos were in black and white, but colour film was introduced in the 1930s.

2 Combustion engine   Imagine if there were no cars, motorbikes, lorries or buses! The combustion engine was invented by a German, Nikolaus Otto, in 1878. And another German, Karl Benz, built the first car in 1885 using Otto's new engine. In 1888, his wife Bertha was the first long-distance driver of this three-wheeled car. She drove their teenage sons on a 106-kilometre trip. It was a long journey because the car went at 16 km an hour! And Bertha had to repair the car during the trip!

3 Light bulb   Is it getting dark? Well, turn on the light! The first successful light bulb was invented in 1879 by the American inventor, Thomas Edison. A light bulb is a glass bulb which is filled with gas and has a thin wire inside it. The wires in the earlier light bulbs burnt quickly, so Edison tried thousands of different wires before he found the right one! Edison is also famous for developing the world's first electric lighting system, which was in New York.

4 Laser   When you play a DVD or a CD, buy things at a cash desk, download music or send an email you are using a laser. Albert Einstein predicted laser technology, but it was developed 40 years later in 1960 by an American called Theodore Maiman. A laser is a concentrated beam of light and it has thousands of uses in medicine, computing, industry, astronomy and medicine. In future lasers may help us produce solar energy.

5 Antibiotics   If we're ill with an infection, the doctor gives us antibiotics. They are a miracle drug. Antibiotics are a living substance which we get from mould. But they were discovered by accident. In 1928, a Scottish scientist called Alexander Fleming noticed that mould killed bacteria in his laboratory. He realised that they could cure illnesses, and made a medicine called penicillin.

2 Read the article and complete the table.

Invention or discovery	Inventor(s) & nationality	Date of invention or discovery
camera	George Eastman, American	1888
combustion engine	Nikolaus Otto,	
car	, German	
	, American	1879
laser	Theodore Maiman,	
	Alexander Fleming,	1928

Listening

3 🔘 **30** Listen and match the teenagers (1–5) with the inventions (a–e).

1 Erika Olsen
2 Michael McMillen
3 Christopher Paradiso
4 Jacqueline Rocchio
5 Nicole Imnesi

a 'Wavetricity-Blue Energy' makes energy from the sea
b 'Sun cream tag' – sun cream monitor
c 'The Booksmart' – an intelligent bookmark
d 'Tech cane' – a GPS stick for people who can't see
e 'Returning Soccer Ball' – finds your football

4 🔘 **30** Listen again and answer the questions.

1 Why did Erika want to help people who can't see? ....
2 What can the bookmark do? ....
3 What were the prizes? ....
4 Which do you think is the best invention? ....

Writing

5 **Make a list of other inventions you think have changed our way of life. For each invention, explain why you think it is important.**

I think that TV is an important invention. It teaches us a lot, and we don't have to leave our homes! We can watch news from around the world, we can also enjoy films and soaps, watch sports events and learn information from documentaries. I can't imagine life without it!

Writing focus

Study the model paragraph carefully before you start. Make sure you give reasons for the inventions you choose.

Your progress

Look at Student's Book Unit 8. Circle: ☺ = not very well ☺ = quite well ☺ = very well

I can ask and answer questions about different kinds of writing.	☺	☺	☺	p78
I can read an article about technology and science and understand the main ideas.	☺	☺	☺	p83
I can understand descriptions of processes and talk about them.	☺	☺	☺	p85
I can use sequencing words such as *firstly*, *secondly*, *then*, *finally* to explain a process.	☺	☺	☺	p85
I can read an article about communication and understand the main points.	☺	☺	☺	p86
I can ask about people's feelings and talk about my own feelings.	☺	☺	☺	p115

Your project: my diary

• Write a diary every day for two weeks.
• Get an exercise book. Stick your favourite pictures on the cover and write *My diary* on it.
• Use a page for each day. Write:
  the date
  a general account of your day
  something that happened
  how you felt
  a star rating   1 = not very exciting   5 = excellent
• Draw a picture for each day or stick in a photo.

1 Read the clues and complete the crossword.

CLUES

1 Nelson Mandela was the president of this country.
2 The capital city of this country is Ankara.
3 There are 50 states in this country.
4 This is the largest country in the world. It has got coasts on three oceans.
5 About 300 languages are spoken here. An official language is Mandarin.
6 This country has four main islands. Its highest mountain is Mount Fuji.
7 Aborigines arrived in this country about 50,000 years ago.
8 This is the largest country in South America. It has got a fantastic football team.
9 This country is next to China and Pakistan.
10 The Olmec, Mayan, Toltec and Aztec civilisations were in this country.

2 🔘 **31** Read the conversation and ⭕(circle) the correct words. Then listen and check.

Toby I'm doing a quiz in this magazine. You've got some free time, ¹ **don't you / haven't you**?

Mia Sure. How can I help?

Toby I want to check some answers. Sydney's the capital of Australia, ² **isn't it / aren't they**?

Mia No. Canberra's the capital city.

Toby Penguins live at the North Pole, ³ **aren't they / don't they**?

Mia No, they don't. They live at the South Pole.

Toby Oh, OK. Jacqueline Wilson writes books, ⁴ **isn't she / doesn't she**?

Mia That's right. She wrote the Tracy Beaker books. Have you finished?

Toby No, there's one more. Elephants can swim, ⁵ **don't they / can't they**?

Mia That's right.

Toby OK, thanks, Mia.

Chat zone

🔘 **32** Complete the conversations with the expressions. Then listen and check.

No problem. I'm starving! You bet!

1 Sara I've bought a big chocolate cake.
Tom Really?
Sara Would you like some?
Tom Yes, please.
....

2 Lucy Hey, I've got an extra ticket for the concert tonight. Do you want to come with me?
Olivia ....

3 Josh Do you want to play tennis later?
Nick I'm sorry, I can't. I have to meet my sister.
Josh ....
What about tomorrow?
Nick That'll be great.

Tag questions

1 Match the statements with the question tags.

1 The sun rises in the East,

2 You live in a flat,

3 He plays for Manchester United,

4 Millie can speak Russian,

5 They've got a new car,

6 Santiago is in Chile,

7 We can swim in the sea,

8 Your parents like old films,

9 Leon is in your class,

10 Your mobile's got a video camera,

a haven't they?

b can't she?

c hasn't it?

d doesn't he?

e isn't it?

f doesn't it?

g can't we?

h don't they?

i don't you?

j isn't he?

2 Put the words in the correct order to make questions. Then match the questions with the pictures.

1 we / , / we / can't / climb down / ? / can _We can climb down, can't we?_

2 aren't / big / my / too / they / trainers / , / , / ? / are ....

3 a / has got / , / new / ? / hasn't / car / Gerry / he ....

4 your house / some / there / food / in / , / , / ? / is / there / isn't ....

5 ? / mother's / a / , / , / isn't / doctor / your / she ....

6 dad / he / collects / , / , / your / doesn't / comics / ? ....

7 ? / late / , / , / for / aren't / we're / the / party / we ....

8 , / you / you / can / can't / ? / a plane / fly ....

a

b 1

c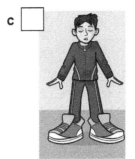

d

e

f

g

h

3 Complete the sentences.

1 You're sixteen, _aren't you_ ?

2 The film starts at 8.30, ... ?

3 They've got a beautiful pet parrot, ... ?

4 She lives near the school, ... ?

5 Your sister is working in New Zealand, ... ?

6 Olivia is a very popular girl's name, ... ?

7 Jake's got short dark hair, ... ?

8 Your parents are out shopping, ... ?

4 Write the journalists' questions.

Your name's Cameron, isn't it?

You live in Hollywood, don't you?

1 you / be / Brazilian

You're Brazilian, aren't you?

2 you / can speak / Spanish

....

3 you / live / in Berlin

....

4 you / have got / two sisters

....

5 you / like / dancing

....

6 your parents / have got / three cars

....

7 you / write / a blog

....

8 you / can fly / a plane

....

9 your uncle / be / an actor

....

10 you / play / basketball

....

5 Answer the journalists' questions for you. Correct them if they are wrong.

1 _Yes, I am. / No, I'm not. I'm Spanish._

2 ....

3 ....

4 ....

5 ....

6 ....

7 ....

8 ....

9 ....

10 ....

6 Write tag questions about Omar. Use the verbs in brackets.

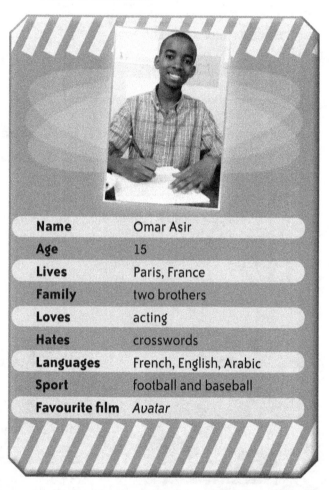

Name	Omar Asir
Age	15
Lives	Paris, France
Family	two brothers
Loves	acting
Hates	crosswords
Languages	French, English, Arabic
Sport	football and baseball
Favourite film	Avatar

1 _His name's Omar Asir, isn't it?_ (be)

2 .... ? (be)

3 .... ? (live)

4 .... ? (have got)

5 .... ? (love)

6 .... ? (hate)

7 .... ? (speak)

8 .... ? (play)

9 .... ? (be)

1 Unscramble the words and label the pictures.

| reyuvintis | tropss netrec | rat lygreal | tanterrusa | ~~éfac~~ |

| hatteer | gonpipsh creent | maidsut | seatcl | thiolspa |

1 ......café...... 2 .... 3 .... 4 .... 5 ....

6 .... 7 .... 8 .... 9 .... 10 ....

2 Match the places from Exercise 1 with the sentences.

a I saw a really exciting match here on Saturday. ...10...

b We're going to see *Hamlet* there at the weekend. ....

c The King lived here for 15 years. ....

d I use the exercise machines and the swimming pool. ....

e What would you like for your dessert? ....

f I don't like these paintings. I don't understand them. ....

g Can I have a smoothie and a chocolate muffin, please? ....

h I fell off my bike and broke my leg. I hope to go home tomorrow. ....

i I'm studying history and philosophy. It's cool! ....

j I love it. You can find every shop here. And it's always warm! ....

3 Imagine you go to the Bluestream Sports Centre. Answer the questions. You can use the words in brackets for ideas.

Bluestream Sports Centre – Customer survey

1 When do you usually come here? (after college)
I usually come here after college. I sometimes come here at the weekend, too.

2 Why do you come to this sports centre? (to get fit) ....

3 Who do you come with? (a friend) ....

4 How often do you come here? (twice a week) ....

5 What do you usually do here? (go swimming) ....

6 Why do you like it? (meet friends / nice atmosphere) ....

7 How would you improve the sports centre? (make the café bigger)

....

8 Which do you prefer, the sports centre or the park? Why? (the sports centre / lots to do)

....

Thank you for your help.

Question words review

1 Match the questions and answers.

1 What was Van Gogh's first name?
2 Why do you look so sad?
3 What were you doing when I called last night?
4 How much are the tickets?
5 How do you go to school?
6 When did you get back from your holiday?
7 Who were you talking to at lunchtime?
8 How often do you send text messages?
9 Where did you put my bag, Mum?
10 How many pairs of trainers have you got?

a In your room.
b About 30 times a day.
c I was at the gym. I had training.
d I don't know. Maybe seven?
e Vincent.
f Because I've lost my mobile phone.
g A new student in my class.
h I usually go by bike.
i 15 euros.
j Last week.

2 Put the words in the correct order to make questions. Then write answers for you.

1 do / did / what / last weekend / you / ? _What did you do last weekend?_

2 your last holiday / where / did / go / you / on / ? ....

3 send / do / text messages / how often / you / ? ....

4 you / do / who / the most / admire / ? ....

5 did / your best friend / you / meet / when / ? ....

3 Write the questions for the answers. Use the question words in the speech bubbles.

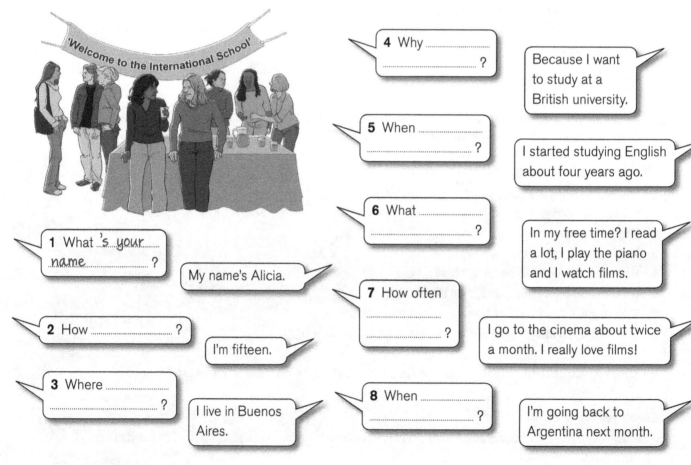

'Welcome to the International School'

4 Why ....
.... ?

Because I want to study at a British university.

5 When ....
.... ?

I started studying English about four years ago.

6 What ....
.... ?

In my free time? I read a lot, I play the piano and I watch films.

1 What _'s your_ _name_ ?

My name's Alicia.

7 How often ....
.... ?

I go to the cinema about twice a month. I really love films!

2 How .... ?

I'm fifteen.

3 Where ....
.... ?

I live in Buenos Aires.

8 When ....
.... ?

I'm going back to Argentina next month.

Subject and object questions

4 Reorder the words to make questions. Then ⬭circle the correct answers.

1 flew / in / who / this plane / ?

Who flew in this plane?

a The Williams Sisters **ⓑ**The Wright Brothers **c** The Wrong Brothers

2 built / who / this wall / ?

....

a the Russians **b** the Germans **c** the Chinese

3 was / Archimedes / who / ?

....

a an ancient Greek scientist **b** a cartoon superhero **c** a Brazilian footballer

4 was / the South Pole / the first / to reach / person / who / ?

....

a Mr Anderson **b** Roald Amundsen **c** Roald Dahl

5 invented / the sandwich / who / ?

....

a The Lord of the Rings **b** Edward Scissorhands **c** The Earl of Sandwich

6 created / who / Mickey Mouse / ?

....

a Walt Disney **b** Bart Simpson **c** Leonard da Vinci

5 Read Emily's diary. Then write questions for the answers.

Sunday 14 March It was my birthday yesterday – but my party was terrible! Amelie talked to Sofia but she didn't talk to me. Lisa danced with Jonny and Sam. Luke argued with Brendon. Mia didn't talk to Nick. Kevin watched TV all the time. And Harry didn't come at all!

1 ....Who talked to Sofia?....... Amelie
2 .... Jonny and Sam
3 .... Brendon
4 .... Nick
5 .... Kevin
6 .... Harry

Communication

◉ **33** Complete the conversations. Then listen and check.

problem   floor   is   all   miss   up   take   right   turn   ~~where~~

A

Sam Excuse me. Can you tell me ¹.......where....... the internet café is, please?
Louise Yes, of course. Go ².......................... the stairs to the first floor. It's on the left, next to the restaurant.
Sam So it's on the first ³.......................... on the left?
Louise That's ⁴.......................... .
Sam Thank you.
Louise Not at ⁵.......................... .

B

Stan Excuse me. ⁶.......................... there a book shop here?
Ron Yes, there is. ⁷.......................... the lift to the third floor.
Stan The third floor?
Ron That's right. Then ⁸.......................... left. It's on your right, between the pharmacy and the games shop. You can't ⁹.......................... it!
Stan Thanks very much.
Ron No ¹⁰.......................... .

Reading

1 Read the article and match the numbers with the information.

1	1965	**a**	the number of underground cities in Cappadocia
2	333 BC	**b**	the number of years ago people first came to Cappadocia
3	40	**c**	the number of floors in Derinkuyu
4	10,000	**d**	the year people could visit Derinkuyu
5	36	**e**	the height in metres of some 'fairy chimneys'
6	7	**f**	the year Cappadocia was invaded by Alexander the Great

Incredible Cappadocia

There are strange towers of rock. There are mysterious caves. There are cities under the ground. At one time, George Lucas wanted to film some parts of *Star Wars* here. But these amazing places aren't on an alien planet. They are in Cappadocia in central Turkey.

Nature and 'Man' created this incredible landscape. Nature formed the 'fairy chimneys' which cover the region. These are tall towers of soft rock with a 'hat' of hard rock on the top. Some of them are 40m tall. But people built the tunnels and underground cities.

People first came here 10,000 years ago. Different empires ruled here, including the Hittites (from 3,500 BC) and the Persians. Alexander the Great came here in 333 BC and the Romans in 63 BC. There were lots of invasions and Cappadocia could be a dangerous place. People wanted to feel safe, so they started building their homes underground.

There are 36 underground cities in Cappadocia. The largest is at Derinkuyu. It was built under a hill. It covers an area of four square kilometres. The underground city was built on seven floors and was 85 metres below the surface. There were homes, kitchens, churches, stables for horses and meeting halls. There was even a prison! Derinkuyu Underground City was opened to the public in 1965. The second largest city is at Kaymakly, nine kilometres away. A two-metre wide underground tunnel connects the two cities!

People first started building these underground cities nearly 3,000 years ago. They also built their homes in the fairy chimneys, sometimes up to five floors. In fact, some of these homes are still lived in today and tourists can stay in them.

Cappadocia is now a World Heritage Site and an important centre of tourism. You can explore some of the caves and underground cities. You can even travel over this fantastic landscape in a hot-air balloon!

2 Read the article again. Are the sentences true (*T*) or false (*F*)? Correct the false information.

1 The 'fairy chimneys' were built by people. ..F..
2 The Romans invaded Cappadocia after Alexander the Great. ....
3 People lived underground because they wanted to be safe. ....
4 Derinkuyu was built near a hill. ....
5 Kaymakly is not as big as Derinkuyu. ....
6 People started building the underground cities 3,500 years ago. ....

Listening

3 ◉ **34** **Listen to the tourist guide and answer the questions with numbers.**

1 In which year was Pompeii destroyed? ....

2 How many people lived here? ....

3 How many cities were destroyed by Mount Vesuvius? ....

4 When was Pompeii discovered again? ....

5 How many tourists go there every year? ....

4 ◉ **34** **Listen again and complete the tourist guide's notes.**

> Pompeii was destroyed by a ¹.. .
> It was a typical Roman ².. .
> Pompeii was a port and ³.. came from all over the world.
> It was a nice place to live and lots of Romans had holiday ⁴.. here.
> It was destroyed on 24th ⁵.. AD 79.
> Pompeii was forgotten for about ⁶.. years.
> Now it's a very popular place for ⁷.. .

Writing

5 **Write about another famous ancient city. It can be in your country or anywhere in the world. Write about:**

- where it is
- when it was built and when people lived there
- why it is famous
- some important buildings
- what it is like today

Writing focus

Before you write, make notes about the information. Check your facts in books or on the internet. After you write, don't forget to check your spelling!

Your progress

Look at Student's Book Unit 9. Circle: ☺ = not very well ☺ = quite well 😃 = very well

I can ask and answer questions to check information using tag questions.	☺ ☺ 😃	p90 p91
I can read and understand an article about shopping centres and respond with my own ideas.	☺ ☺ 😃	p93
I can comfortably use questions in a range of tenses to have a conversation.	☺ ☺ 😃	p94
I can read and understand the information in an article about cities.	☺ ☺ 😃	p96
I can listen and understand the main points in a discussion about cities.	☺ ☺ 😃	p97
I can ask for and give directions inside a big building such as a shopping centre.	☺ ☺ 😃	p116

Your project: my 60-second interview

- Use the questions below to prepare a questionnaire. Write your own answers.

What's ... the last present you were given? the last sport you played? your most disliked food?

What ... are you wearing now? did you do on your last birthday? do you want to do when you grow up?

Where ... is your favourite place to relax? would you like to visit in the world?

Who's ... your hero? your favourite family member?

- Take your answers to school and share them with your partner. Are any of your answers the same?

1 Complete the crossword with the items.

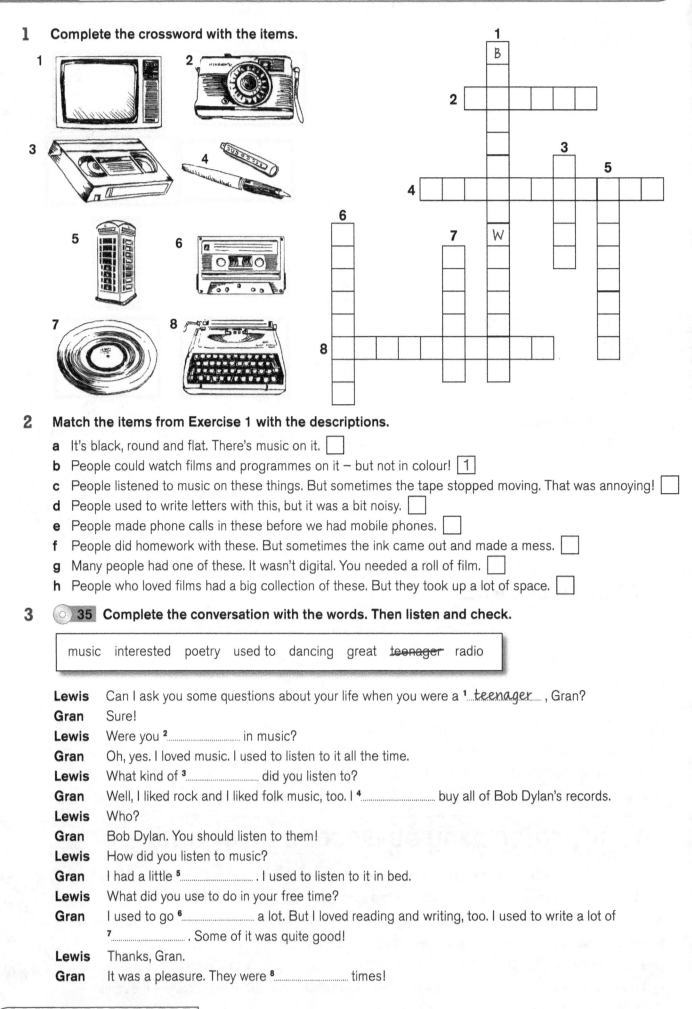

2 Match the items from Exercise 1 with the descriptions.

a It's black, round and flat. There's music on it. ☐

b People could watch films and programmes on it – but not in colour! ☐1

c People listened to music on these things. But sometimes the tape stopped moving. That was annoying! ☐

d People used to write letters with this, but it was a bit noisy. ☐

e People made phone calls in these before we had mobile phones. ☐

f People did homework with these. But sometimes the ink came out and made a mess. ☐

g Many people had one of these. It wasn't digital. You needed a roll of film. ☐

h People who loved films had a big collection of these. But they took up a lot of space. ☐

3 ○ **35** Complete the conversation with the words. Then listen and check.

> music   interested   poetry   used to   dancing   great   ~~teenager~~   radio

Lewis Can I ask you some questions about your life when you were a ¹ ..teenager.. , Gran?

Gran Sure!

Lewis Were you ² .... in music?

Gran Oh, yes. I loved music. I used to listen to it all the time.

Lewis What kind of ³ .... did you listen to?

Gran Well, I liked rock and I liked folk music, too. I ⁴ .... buy all of Bob Dylan's records.

Lewis Who?

Gran Bob Dylan. You should listen to them!

Lewis How did you listen to music?

Gran I had a little ⁵ .... I used to listen to it in bed.

Lewis What did you use to do in your free time?

Gran I used to go ⁶ .... a lot. But I loved reading and writing, too. I used to write a lot of ⁷ .... Some of it was quite good!

Lewis Thanks, Gran.

Gran It was a pleasure. They were ⁸ .... times!

used to

1 **Match the activities with the pictures. Then write sentences.**

make cakes / work in a top restaurant

have frightening dreams / write horror stories

read comics / direct action movies

argue all the time / be married

~~play violin / play the piano~~

throw paper planes / fly a plane

1 THEN — NOW

He used to play the violin but now he plays the piano.

4 THEN — NOW

2 THEN — NOW

5 THEN — NOW

3 THEN — NOW

6 THEN — NOW

2 **Complete Justin's blog. Use *used to* / *didn't use to* and the verbs in brackets.**

My university life
by Justin

Hi there!

Well, here I am at university. It's 200km from my home, so I'm living in student accommodation. I like living away from home. But listen, guys. Life at university isn't easy!

My parents ¹ ..... *used to cook* ..... (cook) all my meals. Now I have to cook them all myself. But my parents didn't only cook my meals. They ² .... (do) a lot of other things as well! Now I have to decide what to eat, then I have to go shopping, next I have to cook, and finally I have to do the dishes. That's hard!

When I lived at home, I ³ .... (wash) my clothes. I ⁴ .... (put) my dirty things in the clothes basket, or just leave them on the floor. I know, I know, that's terrible. But now I have to go to the launderette and wash my own clothes. That's boring.

Another thing. I ⁵ .... (make) my bed. That was lazy. But now I have to make my bed every morning (well, every afternoon!).

My parents ⁶ .... (tell) me to do my homework. They ⁷ .... (ask) things like, 'Have you done your homework yet? Have you started your homework? Did you remember to do your homework?' Now I have to think about all these things on my own.

At home, I ⁸ .... (need) an alarm clock in the mornings. My mum ⁹ .... (wake) me up. Or my little sister. But now? That's right. I have to get up on my own and there's nobody here to help me.

Don't get me wrong. I love being at university. But my life ¹⁰ .... (be) a lot easier at home!

3 How did people live 100 years ago? Write positive and negative sentences.

1 They didn't use to talk on mobile phones.
They used to write letters.

2 _____

3 _____

4 _____

5 _____

6 _____

1 talk on mobile phones
2 listen to music on mp3 players
3 eat junk food
4 go to the cinema
5 travel long distances by plane
6 wear jeans and T-shirts

used to – questions

4 Complete the conversation with *used to*, *didn't use to* or *use to*.

Maddy Grandad, is it true you used to live in Australia when you were a kid?

Grandad Yes. We moved there when I was only five, and we stayed there for three years.

Maddy Where did you ¹ __use to__ live? Did you live in a city?

Grandad No, we ² _____ live in a city. We lived in a small town called Semaphore in South Australia. It was near the coast.

Maddy Did you ³ _____ live in a big house?

Grandad No, we didn't. We ⁴ _____ live in a bungalow. It had a metal roof. I remember the noise it ⁵ _____ make when it rained. I ⁶ _____ like that. It was frightening!

Maddy What did you ⁷ _____ do at the weekends?

Grandad My father had a boat. We all ⁸ _____ go sailing on the sea. It was fantastic.

Maddy Could you swim?

Grandad Yes, I could. I ⁹ _____ swim a lot in the sea. But we had to be careful because sometimes there were sharks!

Maddy Was your life very different in Australia than in England?

Grandad Well, the biggest difference, was the weather. It was much hotter in Australia. We ¹⁰ _____ eat our Christmas dinner at home. We ¹¹ _____ have a picnic on the beach. That was strange!

5 Write more questions to ask Maddy's grandad. Use the words below.

1 where / go to school?
Where did you use to go to school?

2 what games / play?

3 what time / start school in the morning?

4 have / a best friend?

5 what / do in the school holidays?

6 Unscramble the questions. Then write answers for you.

1 to school / use to / a bike / you / ride / did ?
Did you use to ride a bike to school?
No, I used to walk to school.

2 have / you / did / a special toy / use to ?

3 use to / lunch / did / at school / have / you ?

4 go / you / did / to bed / use to / what time ?

5 did / what / use to / you / in your free time / do ?

1 Read the instructions and find the words.

O	F	F	E	R	T	A	E	C	Y	T	U	N	C
N	E	I	V	A	T	C	O	M	E	D	Y	R	O
N	U	R	S	E	T	E	A	C	H	E	R	T	U
U	N	E	A	A	V	G	H	T	E	R	U	S	S
R	C	F	T	U	N	C	L	E	W	E	R	H	I
S	C	I	E	N	C	E	F	I	C	T	I	O	N
E	M	G	O	T	H	E	M	D	E	R	T	R	O
O	H	H	D	E	A	F	S	E	R	I	O	R	T
I	S	T	E	P	F	A	T	H	E	R	P	O	P
M	C	E	F	A	E	N	G	I	N	E	E	R	R
O	Z	R	E	A	D	T	B	R	A	T	H	E	R
U	A	C	T	O	D	A	U	G	H	T	E	R	I
S	I	S	T	M	U	S	I	C	A	L	N	I	C
E	A	S	L	A	W	Y	E	R	T	E	A	C	H

FIND ...

FIVE JOBS (THEY BEGIN WITH THE LETTERS *T, F, N, L* AND *E*)

FIVE FAMILY MEMBERS (THEY BEGIN WITH THE LETTERS *C, A, D, S* AND *U*)

FIVE FILM GENRES (THEY BEGIN WITH THE LETTERS *C, F, M, H* AND *S*)

...IN THE WORD SQUARE.

2 Complete the questions with the words.

(going) (today) (another) (read) (too)

(rainy) (Sunday) (~~free~~) (visit) (go)

1 What would you do if you had more ....free.... time?
2 What was the last book you .... ?
3 What are you .... to do later?
4 Where would you .... if you could travel in time?
5 Do you ever .... websites in English?
6 What will you do if it's .... on Saturday?
7 What do you have .... much of?
8 Have you ever been to .... country?
9 What were you doing at 11 a.m. on .... ?
10 What have you already done .... ?

3 Match the questions from Exercise 2 with the answers.

a Yes, I do. I visit the sites of my favourite bands. And they're mainly American. ☐
b I'd go to Ancient Egypt in the time of the pharaohs. ☐
c Yes, I have. I've been to Canada and Brazil. ☐
d I think it was *Stormbreaker* with Alex Rider. He's great! ☐
e I have too much homework! ☐
f I'd learn to play the piano. That would be cool! [1]
g I was tidying my room. Boring! ☐
h I've already done a lot of school work! ☐
i I'm going to write to my friend in Berlin. ☐
j I'll probably stay at home and sleep! ☐

4 Answer the questions in Exercise 2 for you.

Ⓡ Present perfect

1 Do the questionnaire.

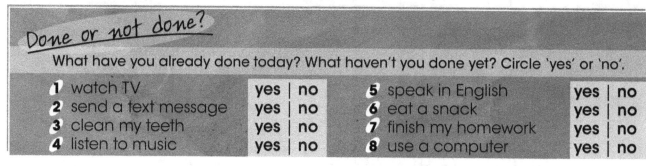

Done or not done?

What have you already done today? What haven't you done yet? Circle 'yes' or 'no'.

1 watch TV	yes | no	
2 send a text message	yes | no	
3 clean my teeth	yes | no	
4 listen to music	yes | no	
5 speak in English	yes | no
6 eat a snack	yes | no
7 finish my homework	yes | no
8 use a computer	yes | no

2 Write sentences about what you *have already done* or *haven't done yet*.

Ⓡ Present perfect and past simple

3 Complete the article with the correct form of the verbs in brackets.

Explorer profile: A busy man!

Robin Hanbury-Tenison is an explorer and author. He ¹ ..... *has been* ..... (go) on many incredible journeys in his life. He ² .... (walk) thousands of kilometres. He ³ .... (sail) all sorts of boats, and ⁴ .... (ride) horses and camels in many different countries. In fact he ⁵ .... (go) on more than 30 expeditions.

In 1958 he ⁶ .... (be) the first person to cross South America at its widest point – 5,000 kilometres! Then he ⁷ .... (travel) across the Sahara between 1962 and 1966 and ⁸ .... (meet) tribal people there.

His wife is also a great adventurer. In 1984 they ⁹ .... (ride) 1,600 kilometres across France. In 1989 they even ¹⁰ .... (take) their young son, Merlin, on a long expedition to Spain.

Robin ¹¹ .... (write) many books about his adventures. He ¹² .... (work) all his life to protect tribal people. He is the president of Survival International.

Ⓡ First conditional

4 Write the verbs in the correct tense.

1 If my teacher ..... *doesn't give* ..... (not give) us homework, I ..... *will be* ..... (be) really happy!

2 If my dog .... (break) anything in the house, I .... (pay) for it.

3 My sister .... (not go) on the picnic if it .... (be) cold tomorrow.

4 If we .... (stay) at home tonight, I .... (make) the dinner. Really!

5 If my friends .... (have) a problem, I .... (try) to help them.

6 If I .... (go) to bed very late tonight, I .... (feel) terrible tomorrow.

Ⓡ Second conditional

5 Circle the correct answers.

1 If I **would break** / (**broke**) my leg, I (**would go**) / **went** to hospital.

2 Eric **would be** / **was** happy if his parents **would buy** / **bought** him a car.

3 If you **would** / **could** travel in time, what year **would** / **did** you visit?

4 We **would go** / **went** to New York if we **would have** / **had** the opportunity.

5 If I **would** / **could** sing well, I **would enter** / **entered** a competition.

Reported speech

6 Read the telephone conversations and then complete the notes.

1 Eva   Hi. Is Megan there?
    Dad   No, I'm sorry. She's out.
    Eva   It's Eva. Can you tell her I'm sailing in the Mediterranean? Thanks.

2 Daisy   Hi, it's Daisy. Is Megan there?
    Dad   No, I'm sorry.
    Daisy   Can she call me? I'm waiting for her outside the cinema.

3 Lily   Hi, Megan!
    Dad   I'm sorry, Megan isn't here. I'm her father.
    Lily   Can you tell her Lily and Lucy called? We're baking a cake. It's her favourite!

4 Josh   Hi, it's Josh here. Can I speak to Megan?
    Dad   I'm afraid she isn't here.
    Josh   Can you ask her to call me? I need help with my homework.

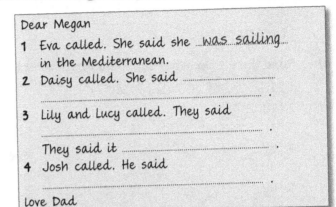

Dear Megan

1 Eva called. She said she ...was sailing... in the Mediterranean.
2 Daisy called. She said ....
3 Lily and Lucy called. They said ....
   They said it ....
4 Josh called. He said ....

love Dad

7   Report the questions.

1   'Does your dog enjoy exercise?'
Holly ....

'Are you waiting for me?'
Sara asked *if she was waiting for her* .

2

3

'Are you enjoying your meal?'
The waiter ....

Communication

🔊 36   **Complete the conversations. Then listen and check.**

home   afraid   going   see   touch   safe   coming   ~~time~~   goodbye   call

A
Gran   Bye, Emma. It's ¹ .....time..... for me to go.
Emma   Bye, Gran. Have a ² .... journey.
Gran   Thanks, Emma.
Emma   ³ .... me when you get ⁴ ....

B
Luke   Bye, Matt. I'm ⁵ .... I have to go.
Matt   Thanks for ⁶ .... I hope you enjoyed the party.
Luke   ⁷ .... you at school tomorrow.

C
Jessica   I've come to say ⁸ .... , Ellen.
Ellen   I'm ⁹ .... to miss you.
Jessica   Keep in ¹⁰ .... !

Reading

1 Read the article. What do the numbers refer to?

1 12 ... She met 12 American presidents. ....

2 1882 ....

3 11 ....

4 87 ....

5 30 ....

6 39 ....

Helen Keller, a true superstar

Helen Keller is famous because she changed the lives of many people. She had a dream. She wanted people with disabilities to live normal lives and she worked for that goal all her life. But Helen's achievements were amazing because she was deaf and blind. When she was born in 1880, people like her didn't have opportunities or help.

When Helen Keller was born in a small farm town in Tuscumbia, Alabama, she was a happy, healthy girl. But only nineteen months later, in the winter of 1882, she got ill with a fever. Helen survived the illness – but it left her deaf and blind. She couldn't hear music or birds singing or her parents' voices. And she couldn't see faces, animals, trees or the sun.

Helen became a difficult child. She used to grow angry and frustrated with her parents. It was impossible for them to communicate. She was very unhappy. So her parents asked a teacher called Anne Sullivan to help. Anne quickly taught Helen how to spell words with her hands. But there was a problem – Helen couldn't understand what the words meant. Then one day, Anne took Helen into the garden and held one of her hands under a water pump.

Then she spelled the word 'water' into Helen's other hand. At last, Helen understood the connection. Her mind opened up to a new world and that day she learned 30 new words.

Helen was very clever. She learned German, French, Latin and Greek! She met 12 American presidents and she wrote 11 books. Her first book, called *The Story of My Life*, was a bestseller and it was translated into 50 languages. Helen helped raise money for organisations such as the American Federation for the Blind. She campaigned for the rights of the blind in 39 countries in five continents. People always wanted to hear about her experiences. Helen died in her sleep aged 87 in 1968.

Helen's life was an inspiration to other people and two Oscar-winning films were made about her life. She was a true superstar!

2 Read the article again. Are the sentences true (*T*) or false (*F*)?

1 She was 19 when she became deaf and blind. ... F

2 Anne Sullivan offered to help Helen's parents. ....

3 Anne helped Helen understand the meaning of new words. ....

4 Helen's first book wasn't a big success. ....

5 Helen travelled all over the world to help the blind. ....

6 Two films about Helen won Oscars. ....

Listening

3 🔘 **37** Listen and number the stories in the correct order.

a

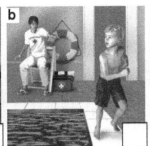
b

c

d

e

4 🔘 **37** Listen again and answer the questions.

Jamie Lola David Alisha Tom

1 Who started laughing? ....
2 Who heard a very loud noise? ....
3 Who was upset and started crying? .... and ....
4 Who was very happy? ....
5 Who saw an accident? ....

Writing

5 Write a paragraph about your first memory.
Think about these questions and make notes.

How old were you? Where were you? Who was with you?
What happened? What did you see and hear? How did you feel?

Writing focus
When you write about an experience, make your story interesting for the reader. Use adjectives and adverbs to make it more exciting.

Your progress

Look at Student's Book Unit 10. Circle: ☹ = not very well ☺ = quite well 😎 = very well

I can understand an article about someone's life when they were young.	☹	☺	😎	p99
I can talk about past routines and habits.	☹	☺	😎	p101
I can talk about a range of everyday topics without planning what I am going to say.	☹	☺	😎	p103
I can read an article about Carlos Acosta and understand the main points and details.	☹	☺	😎	p106
I can listen to people talking about their childhood and understand the gist.	☹	☺	😎	p107
I can write a biography of someone, describing them and their early life.	☹	☺	😎	p107
I can say goodbye in a variety of situations including when someone goes on a journey.	☹	☺	😎	p117

Your project: a Nobel Prize winner

- Prepare a computer or poster presentation about a Nobel Prize winner.
- Find information and pictures from the internet or books. Include:
  name, job and basic biography (birth date, nationality, family, etc.)
  the person's career achievements
  why they won the Nobel Prize
  why you admire the person
- Give your presentation to the class.

Past simple and past continuous

Unit 1

Past simple

Positive		Negative		
I / He / She / It / We / You / They	worked. ate.	I / He / She / It / We / You / They	did not didn't	work. eat.

Questions and short answers						
Did	I / he / she / it / we / you / they	work? eat?	Yes, No,	I / he / she / it / we / you / they	did. didn't.	

We use the past simple to talk about finished events or actions in the past:

*I **went** to the cinema last night. John **didn't come** home early yesterday.*
***Did** you **see** Maya on Saturday? Yes, I **did**.*

Add **-d/-ed** to make the past simple of most regular verbs: *live* ⟶ *lived*, *start* ⟶ *started*
Many verbs are irregular in the past and do not add **-ed**: *give* ⟶ **gave**, *eat* ⟶ **ate**

Past continuous

Positive and negative			Questions and short answers					
I / He / She / It	was was not wasn't	sleeping.	Was	I / he / she / it	sleeping?	Yes,	I / he / she / it	was.
						No,	I / he / she / it	wasn't.
We / You / They	were were not weren't		Were	we / you / they		Yes,	we / you / they	were.
						No,	we / you / they	weren't.

We use the past continuous to talk about actions in progress in the past:

*The people **were waiting** for the train. I **wasn't listening** to Beyoncé.*
***Was** the girl **running** too fast? Yes, she **was**.*

when/while

Unit 1

We use **when/while** + past continuous or past simple to talk about a long action in the past which was interrupted by a short action.
We use **while** or **when** + past continuous to introduce the long action:
***While/When** we **were playing** basketball it started to rain.*
We use **when** + past simple to introduce the short action:
*I was having a shower **when** you **phoned**.*

must / have to

Unit 1

Positive	I / He / She / It / We / You / They	must / have to	go.
Negative	I / He / She / It / We / You / They	mustn't / don't have to	go.

We use **must/mustn't** and **have to** + verb to talk about rules and obligations:
*You **must**/**have to** be quiet in the library. We **mustn't** use our mobile phones at school.*
We use **don't have to** + verb when an action is not necessary:
*We **don't have to** go to school tomorrow.*
We usually use *have to*, not *must*, in questions:
*Do we **have to** get up early tomorrow?*
The past of *must* and *have to* is **had to**:
*We **had to** help Dad in the garden yesterday.*

will/won't • definitely/probably

Positive and negative		
I / He / She / It / We / You / They	will	eat.
I / He / She / It / We / You / They	will not won't	eat.

Questions and short answers					
Will	I / he / she / it / we / you / they	eat?	Yes,	I / he / she / it / we / you / they	will.
			No,	I / he / she / it / we / you / they	won't.

We use **will/won't** + verb to make predictions about the future:
I will learn French next year. It won't rain tonight. Will robots do the housework in 2025? Yes, they will.
We often use *think / definitely / probably* to make predictions:
I think I'll go on holiday to Florida. (not sure)
It will definitely snow tomorrow. (sure)
They will probably get married in July. (not completely sure)

will for offers, promises and decisions

We use **will/won't** + verb for offers, promises or decisions made at the time of speaking:
A I'm cold. B I'll close the window. (offer)
A Don't be late! B Don't worry. I'll be at the station at five o'clock. (promise)
What shall I do now? I know! I'll visit Gran. (decision)

Present continuous and going to

We use the present continuous to talk about fixed arrangements in the future:
When are you leaving for Paris? I'm leaving on Friday.
We use **am/is/are** + **going to** + verb to talk about future plans and intentions:
He's going to be a doctor when he grows up.

Present perfect

Positive and negative		
I / We / You / They	have	arrived.
	have not haven't.	
He / She / It	has	arrived.
	has not hasn't	

Questions and short answers					
Have	I / we / you / they	arrived?	Yes,	I / we / you / they	have.
			No,		haven't.
Has	he / she / it	arrived?	Yes,	he / she / it	has.
			No,		hasn't.

We use the present perfect to talk generally about our experiences up to now:
I've been to England. They haven't eaten snails. Has she ridden a horse? No, she hasn't.
We do not use the present perfect to talk about an exact moment in the past. We use the past simple:
They ate snails for dinner last night.
We also use the present perfect when there is a result in the present:
I've lost my keys. (Present result: I haven't got the keys NOW.)

Present perfect with for/since

We use the present perfect to talk about situations which started in the past and continue up to now.
We use **for** to talk about a period of time:
for ten minutes, for six weeks, for a month: How long have you had your bike? I've had it for two weeks.
We use **since** to talk about the moment when a situation started:
since 2011, since last Sunday, since my birthday: I haven't seen Eliza since last weekend.

Present perfect and past simple

Unit 3

We often start a conversation in the present perfect to talk about past experiences in general:
The best place I've ever visited is London.
But we often continue with the past simple to give more information:
We went there last year. I rode on the London Eye and visited Madame Tussauds.
When we use the past simple we often used time expressions: *yesterday, last weekend, two years ago*

Present perfect and *just*

Unit 4

We use the present perfect and **just** to talk about a situation that happened a short time ago:
Your dog's wet. I know. I've just washed him.

Present perfect and already/yet

Unit 4

We use the present perfect and **already** to say that a situation happened sooner than we expect.
She's already finished the English test.
We use **yet** to say that a situation is continuing but we expect it to change.
He hasn't finished his English homework yet.
We use **yet** in questions to ask about a situation we expect to change.
Has he finished his homework yet?

Indefinite pronouns

Unit 4

	people	things	places
some	somebody/someone	something	somewhere
any	anybody/anyone	anything	anywhere
every	everybody/everyone	everything	everywhere
no	nobody/no one	nothing	nowhere

We use indefinite pronouns to talk about people, things or places without saying exactly who, what or where they are:
*There's **someone** here.*
*I don't know **anyone** in my new school.*
*Is there **anything** in the box?*
***Everything** was fine.*
*I looked **everywhere** for the keys.*
***Nobody** goes to school on Sunday.*

too / too much / too many / (not) enough

Unit 4

We use **too** to mean more than is necessary:
*This homework is **too** hard.*
We use **too much** with uncountable nouns and **too many** with countable nouns:
*There's **too much** sugar in this coffee. There are **too many** people here.*
We use **not enough** with countable and uncountable nouns to mean less than is necessary:
*She hasn't got **enough** money to buy the DVD. There aren't **enough** sandwiches.*

Zero conditional

Unit 5

We use the zero conditional to talk about results of facts. We use the present simple in both the condition and the result:
*If you **heat** water to 100°C, it **boils**. If I **get up** late, I **miss** my bus.*

First conditional

Unit 5

We use the first conditional to talk about possible future events.

Condition – *If* + present simple	Result – *will/won't* + verb
If it's sunny tomorrow,	we'll go to the beach.
If it rains this afternoon,	he won't play tennis.

The condition can come before or after the result. Use a comma if the condition comes first:
*If we **are** late, our teacher **won't be** happy. / Our teacher **won't be** happy if we **are** late.*

Defining relative clauses

Unit 5

We use a defining relative clause to say exactly which person, thing or place we mean.

		Pronoun	
People	Anne is the girl	**who/that**	lives next door.
Things	This is the book	**which/that**	I got for my birthday.
Places	The school	**where**	I study is very modern.

Reported speech – statements

Unit 6

When we report what someone said we use a reporting verb and change the tense.

Direct speech		Reported speech	
Present simple	Jack said, 'I **love** cheese.'	**Past simple**	Jack said (that) he **loved** cheese.
am/are/is	Sue said, 'I**'m** thirsty.'	*was/were*	Sue said (that) she **was** thirsty.
have/has got	Sergei said, 'I**'ve got** a headache.'	*had*	Sergei said (that) he **had** a headache.
Present continuous	Maya said, 'Jamie**'s making** dinner.'	**Past continuous**	Maya said (that) Jamie **was making** dinner.
am/are/is going to	Peter said, 'I**'m going to** buy a new game.'	*was/were going to*	Peter said (that) he **was going to** buy a new game.

There are common pronoun and possessive adjective changes in reported speech:
I → he/she   we → they   my → his/her
our → their   me → him/her   us → them
'We're going to take our dog with us.' → ***They*** *said that **they** were going to take **their** dog with **them**.*

Reported speech – modals

Unit 6

Direct speech		Reported speech	
can	Ross said, 'I can skateboard.'	*could*	Ross said (that) he could skateboard.
will	Amy said, 'I will study French at university.'	*would*	Amy said (that) she would study French at university.
must	Pippa said, 'We must eat more vegetables.'	*must / had to*	Pippa said (that) they must / had to eat more vegetables.
have to	Ahmet said, 'I have to go to the doctor's.'	*had to*	Ahmet said (that) he had to go to the doctor's.
mustn't	The teacher said, 'You mustn't drop litter.'	*mustn't*	The teacher said (that) we mustn't drop litter.

Grammar reference

Reported speech – *yes/no* questions Unit 6

When we report *yes/no* questions we use **asked** + **if** and change the tense.
We use the affirmative verb order:
'Is it cold?' → *He **asked if it was** cold.*
'Do you speak English?' → *She **asked if I spoke** English.*

Second conditional statements, questions and short answers Unit 7

Statements	
Condition: *if* + subject + past simple	**Result: subject + *would/wouldn't* + verb**
If I won 1,000 euros,	I'd be very excited.
If she didn't watch TV,	she would have more time.

Questions and short answers		
Result: *would* + subject + verb	**Condition: *if* + subject + past simple**	
Would you have a sports car	if you were famous?	
Yes,	I / he / she / it /	would.
No,	we / you / they	wouldn't.

We use the second conditional to talk about imaginary situations:
*If I **saw** a ghost, I **would be** really scared.* (= But I probably won't see a ghost.)
We can put the condition before or after the result. Use a comma if the condition comes first:
*If you **studied** more, you **would get** better marks. / You **would get** better marks if you **studied** more.*
***Would** Jack **be** healthier if he ate more fruit? / If Jack **ate** more fruit, **would** he **be** healthier?*

Second conditional *wh-* questions Unit 7

Result: *wh-* word + *would* + subject + verb	**Condition: *if* + subject + past simple**
What would you do	if you won the lottery?
Where would you go	if you didn't have school tomorrow?
Who would you take with you	if you won tickets to a concert?

Present passive positive, negative, questions and short answers Unit 8

Positive			Negative			Questions and short answers			
I	am		I	am not / 'm not		Am	I		Yes, I am. / No, I'm not.
He She It	is	driven.	He She It	is not / isn't	driven.	Is	he she it	driven?	Yes, he / she / it is. / No, he / she / it isn't.
We You They	are		We You They	are not / aren't		Are	we you they		Yes, we / you / they are. / No, we / you / they aren't.

We form the passive with **am/is/are** + past participle of the verb.
We use the passive when the person doing the action is not important:
*Breakfast **is served** at 8 am.* (Here we are interested in the time of breakfast, not who serves it.)
We use *by* if we want to say who does the action: *Breakfast **is served** at 8 am **by** the waiters.*

Past passive positive, negative, questions and short answers **Unit 8**

Positive			Negative			Questions and short answers			
I He She It	was	driven.	I He She It	was not wasn't	driven.	Was	I he she it	driven?	Yes, I / he / she / it was. No, I / he / she / it wasn't.
We You They	were		We You They	were not weren't		Were	we you they		Yes, we / you / they were. No, we / you / they weren't.

Tag questions **Unit 9**

We can add a question tag to the end of a statement to make it into a question.

Statement	Question tag
You**'re** French,	**aren't** you?
She**'s** got a guitar,	**hasn't** she?
They**'re** playing basketball,	**aren't** they?
You **live** in Brazil,	**don't** you?
We **can** swim,	**can't** we?

Question words review **Unit 9**

Question word	Auxiliary	Subject	Verb	Other words
Where			put	your bag?
What			eat	for breakfast?
When	did	you	go	on holiday?
Why			phone	Jessica?
Who			meet	last night?
How			travel	to school?

Subject and object questions **Unit 9**

In this question, *who* refers to the **object**:

OBJECT	SUBJECT		SUBJECT		OBJECT
Who	**did**	*Emma*	*Emma*	*met*	*Amy.*
		meet?			

In this question, *who* refers to the **subject**:

SUBJECT	OBJECT	SUBJECT	OBJECT
Who	*basketball?*	*Juan*	*basketball.*
played		*played*	

used to **Unit 10**

We use **used to** + verb to talk about things that happened in our life in the past but are not true in the present:

*I **used to watch** cartoons on TV. Now I watch science-fiction films.*

The negative form is **didn't use to** + verb:

*My sister **didn't use to wear** glasses. Now she does.*

The question form is **Did ... use to** + verb:

*Did you **use to eat** much meat? Yes, I **did**. / No, I **didn't**.*

Irregular verbs

Verb	Past simple	Past participle
be	was/were	been
beat	beat	beaten
become	became	become
begin	began	begun
bite	bit	bitten
break	broke	broken
bring	brought	brought
build	built	built
buy	bought	bought
catch	caught	caught
choose	chose	chosen
come	came	come
cost	cost	cost
cut	cut	cut
do	did	done
drink	drank	drunk
drive	drove	driven
eat	ate	eaten
fall	fell	fallen
feel	felt	felt
fight	fought	fought
find	found	found
fly	flew	flown
forget	forgot	forgotten
get	got	got
give	gave	given
go	went	gone
grow	grew	grown
hang	hung	hung
have	had	had
hear	heard	heard
hit	hit	hit
hold	held	held
keep	kept	kept
know	knew	known

Verb	Past simple	Past participle
leave	left	left
lose	lost	lost
make	made	made
meet	met	met
pay	paid	paid
put	put	put
read	read	read
ride	rode	ridden
ring	rang	rung
run	ran	run
say	said	said
see	saw	seen
sell	sold	sold
send	sent	sent
shake	shook	shaken
sing	sang	sung
sink	sank	sunk
sit	sat	sat
sleep	slept	slept
speak	spoke	spoken
spend	spent	spent
stand	stood	stood
steal	stole	stolen
swim	swam	swum
take	took	taken
teach	taught	taught
tell	told	told
think	thought	thought
understand	understood	understood
upset	upset	upset
wake	woke	woken
wear	wore	worn
win	won	won
write	wrote	written

(n) = noun   (v) = verb
(adj) = adjective
(adv) = adverb
(excl) = exclamation
(det) = determiner
(conj) = conjunction
(expr) = expression
(prep) = preposition
(pron) = pronoun

Unit 1

accident (n) /'æk.sɪ.dənt/
achievement (n) /ə'tʃiːv.mənt/
advert (n) /'æd.vɜːt/
afternoon (n) /ˌɑːf.tə'nuːn/
again (adv) /ə'gen/
ago (adv) /ə'gəʊ/
all (det) /ɔːl/
allow (v) /ə'laʊ/
already (adv) /ɔːl'red.i/
also (adv) /'ɔːl.səʊ/
always (adv) /'ɔːl.weɪz/
another (det) /ə'nʌð.ə/
answer (v) /'ɑːn.sə/
area (n) /'eə.ri.ə/
around (prep) /ə'raʊnd/
arrive (v) /ə'raɪv/
article (n) /'ɑː.tɪ.kəl/
at least (expr) /ət 'liːst/
away (adv) /ə'weɪ/
awesome (adj) /'ɔː.səm/
awful (adj) /'ɔː.fəl/
balloon (n) /bə'luːn/
band (n) /bænd/
beach (n) /biːtʃ/
because (conj) /bɪ'kɒz/
before (prep) /bɪ'fɔː/
beginning (n) /bɪ'gɪn.ɪŋ/
bell (n) /bel/
bin (n) /bɪn/
birthday (n) /'bɜːθ.deɪ/
bite (v) /baɪt/
bookmark (v) /'bʊk.mɑːk/
break (v) /breɪk/
bring (v) /brɪŋ/
buddy (n) /'bʌd.i/
busy (adj) /'bɪz.i/
café (n) /'kæf.eɪ/
cake (n) /keɪk/
call (v) /kɔːl/
cartoon (n) /kɑː'tuːn/
celebrate (v) /'sel.ə.breɪt/
celebration (n) /ˌsel.ə'breɪ.ʃən/
century (n) /'sen.tʃər.i/
chat (v) /tʃæt/
chess (n) /tʃes/
chew (v) /tʃuː/
chocolate (n) /'tʃɒk.lət/
city (n) /'sɪt.i/
comment (v) /'kɒm.ent/
confetti (n) /kən'fet.i/
console (n) /'kɒn.səʊl/
costume (n) /'kɒs.tʃuːm/

crash (v) /kræʃ/
create (v) /kri'eɪt/
crew (n) /kruː/
crystal (n) /'krɪs.təl/
dance (v) /dɑːns/
decade (n) /'dek.eɪd/
designer (n) /dɪ'zaɪ.nə/
dinner (n) /'dɪn.ə/
display (n) /dɪ'spleɪ/
download (v) /ˌdaʊn'ləʊd/
drive (v) /draɪv/
driver (n) /'draɪ.və/
each (det) /iːtʃ/
eat (v) /iːt/
embarrassing (adj)
   /ɪm'bær.ə.sɪŋ/
end (n) /end/
enjoy (v) /ɪn'dʒɔɪ/
ever (adv) /'ev.ə/
every (det) /'ev.ri/
exam (n) /ɪg'zæm/
excuse (n) /ɪk'skjuːs/
experience (v) /ɪk'spɪə.ri.əns/
expert (n) /'ek.spɜːt/
festival (n) /'fes.tɪ.vəl/
finish (v) /'fɪn.ɪʃ/
firework (n) /'faɪə.wɜːk/
first (adj) /'fɜːst/
fitness (n) /'fɪt.nəs/
float (v) /fləʊt/
food (n) /fuːd/
forget (v) /fə'get/
fruit (n) /fruːt/
fun (n) /fʌn/
funny (adj) /'fʌn.i/
garage (n) /'gær.ɑːʒ/
garden (n) /'gɑː.dən/
gather (v) /'gæð.ə/
get (v) /get/
giant (adj) /'dʒaɪ.ənt/
give (v) /gɪv/
goal (n) /gəʊl/
gum (n) /gʌm/
gym (n) /dʒɪm/
hand (n) /hænd/
handwritten (adj)
   /ˌhænd'rɪt.ən/
hard (adj) /hɑːd/
hat (n) /hæt/
health (n) /helθ/
hear (v) /hɪə/
help (v) /help/
hilarious (adj) /hɪ'leə.ri.əs/
hole (n) /həʊl/
holiday (n) /'hɒl.ə.deɪ/
hundreds (n) /'hʌn.drədz/
idea (n) /aɪ'dɪə/
illuminated (adj)
   /ɪ'luː.mɪn.eɪ.tɪd/
illustrator (n) /'ɪl.ə.streɪ.tə/
incredible (adj) /ɪn'kred.ə.bəl/
inhabited (adj) /ɪn'hæb.ɪ.tɪd/
instrument (n) /'ɪn.strə.mənt/
interest (n) /'ɪn.trəst/

inter-school (adj)
   /'ɪn.tə ˌskuːl/
interview (n) /'ɪn.tə.vjuː/
into (prep) /'ɪn.tə/
issue (n) /'ɪʃ.uː/
job (n) /dʒɒb/
join (v) /dʒɔɪn/
junk food (n) /'dʒʌŋk ˌfuːd/
kick (n) /kɪk/
leave (v) /liːv/
library (n) /'laɪ.brər.i/
lifestyle (n) /'laɪf.staɪl/
listen (v) /'lɪs.ən/
loads of (expr) /'ləʊdz ˌəv/
log onto (v) /ˌlɒg 'ɒn.tuː/
look after (v) /ˌlʊk 'ɑːf.tə/
lose (v) /luːz/
magazine (n) /ˌmæg.ə'ziːn/
match (n) /mætʃ/
midnight (n) /'mɪd.naɪt/
millions (n) /'mɪl.jənz/
mistake (n) /mɪ'steɪk/
moment (n) /'məʊ.mənt/
neighbour (n) /'neɪ.bə/
noise (n) /nɔɪz/
notebook (n) /'nəʊt.bʊk/
notice (v) /'nəʊ.tɪs/
novel (n) /'nɒv.əl/
occasional (adj) /ə'keɪ.ʒən.əl/
ocean (n) /'əʊ.ʃən/
online (adv) /ˌɒn'laɪn/
operator (n) /'ɒp.ə.reɪ.tə/
opportunity (n)
   /ˌɒp.ə'tʃuː.nə.ti/
oven (n) /'ʌv.ən/
over (prep) /'əʊ.və/
parade (n) /pə'reɪd/
parent (n) /'peə.rənt/
park (n) /pɑːk/
party (n) /'pɑː.ti/
penalty (n) /'pen.əl.ti/
photographer (n)
   /fə'tɒg.rə.fə/
picture (n) /'pɪk.tʃə/
piece (n) /piːs/
pitch (n) /pɪtʃ/
polite (adj) /pə'laɪt/
post (n) /pəʊst/
practice (n) /'præk.tɪs/
practise (v) /'præk.tɪs/
present (n) /'prez.ənt/
probably (adv) /'prɒb.ə.bli/
really (adv) /'rɪə.li/
receive (v) /rɪ'siːv/
relative (n) /'rel.ə.tɪv/
resolution (n) /ˌrez.əl'uː.ʃən/
rugby (n) /'rʌg.bi/
save (v) /seɪv/
school yard (n) /'skuːl ˌjɑːd/
score (v) /skɔː/
seat (n) /siːt/
shocked (adj) /ʃɒkt/
shout (v) /ʃaʊt/
sing (v) /sɪŋ/
sky (n) /skaɪ/

slipper (n) /'slɪp.ə/
special (adj) /'speʃ.əl/
spend (v) /spend/
steal (v) /stiːl/
still (adv) /stɪl/
strike (v) /straɪk/
take part in (v) /ˌteɪk 'pɑːt ˌɪn/
technical (adj) /'tek.nɪ.kəl/
terrible (adj) /'ter.ə.bəl/
text (v) /tekst/
thousands (n) /'θaʊ.zəndz/
through (prep) /θruː/
throw (v) /θrəʊ/
tired (adj) /taɪəd/
towards (prep) /tə'wɔːdz/
tradition (n) /ˌtrə'dɪʃ.ən/
traditional (adj) /trə'dɪʃ.ən.əl/
trouble (n) /'trʌb.əl/
turn (v) /tɜːn/
unfair (adj) /ʌn'feə/
until (prep) /ən'tɪl/
upload (v) /ʌp'ləʊd/
way (n) /weɪ/
wear (v) /weə/
web (n) /web/
website (n) /'web.saɪt/
webzine (n) /'web.ziːn/
well (expr) /wel/
whole (adj) /həʊl/
wish (n) /wɪʃ/

Unit 2

across (prep) /ə'krɒs/
adapt (v) /ə'dæpt/
advantage (n) /əd'vɑːn.tɪdʒ/
affect (v) /ə'fekt/
air (n) /eə/
amount (n) /ə'maʊnt/
ancient (adj) /'eɪn.ʃənt/
argue (v) /'ɑːg.juː/
believe (v) /bɪ'liːv/
bio fuels (n) /'baɪ.əʊ ˌfjuː.əlz/
building (n) /'bɪl.dɪŋ/
business (n) /'bɪz.nɪs/
camcorder (n) /'kæm.kɔː.də/
carbon dioxide (n) /ˌkɑː.bən
   daɪ'ɒk.saɪd/
carry (v) /'kær.i/
cause (v) /kɔːz/
CD (n) /siː'diː/
certain (adj) /'sɜː.tən/
change (v) /tʃeɪndʒ/
chart (n) /tʃɑːt/
cheap (adj) /tʃiːp/
chemical (n) /'kem.ɪ.kəl/
citizen (n) /'sɪt.ɪ.zən/
clean (adj) /kliːn/
climate (n) /'klaɪ.mət/
close (adj) /kləʊs/
cloudy (adj) /'klaʊ.di/
coal (n) /kəʊl/
cold (adj) /kəʊld/
collect (v) /kə'lekt/
comment (n) /'kɒm.ent/

community (n)
/kəˈmjuː.nə.ti/
completely (adv)
/kəmˈpliːt.li/
compost (n) /ˈkɒm.pɒst/
control (v) /kənˈtrəʊl/
copy (v) /ˈkɒp.i/
corn (n) /kɔːn/
cover (v) /ˈkʌv.ə/
damage (n) /ˈdæm.ɪdʒ/
decide (v) /dɪˈsaɪd/
decision (n) /dɪˈsɪʒ.ən/
definitely (adv) /ˈdef.ɪ.nət.li/
desk (n) /desk/
destination (n)
/ˌdes.tɪˈneɪ.ʃən/
diary (n) /ˈdaɪə.ri/
dictionary (n) /ˈdɪk.ʃən.ər.i/
dietary (adj) /ˈdaɪ.ə.tər.i/
different (adj) /ˈdɪf.ər.ənt/
DVD (n) /ˌdiː.viːˈdiː/
earn (v) /ɜːn/
easily (adv) /ˈiː.zɪ.li/
e-book (n) /ˈiː.bʊk/
eco (adj) /ˈiː.kəʊ/
eco-friendly (adj)
/ˌiː.kəʊˈfrend.li/
ecology (n) /iˈkɒl.ə.dʒi/
education (n) /ˌedʒ.ʊˈkeɪ.ʃən/
electric (adj) /iˈlek.trɪk/
electricity (n) /ˌel.ɪkˈtrɪs.ə.ti/
energy (n) /ˈen.ə.dʒi/
energy-saving (adj) /ˈen.ə.dʒi
ˌseɪv.ɪŋ/
environment (n)
/ɪnˈvaɪə.rən.mənt/
exhibition (n) /ˌek.sɪˈbɪʃ.ən/
extreme (adj) /ɪkˈstriːm/
flood (n) /flʌd/
forecaster (n) /ˈfɔː.kɑːstə/
fortunately (adv)
/ˈfɔː.tʃən.ət.li/
fossil fuel (n) /ˈfɒs.əl ˌfjuː.əl/
global warming (n) /ˌgləʊ.bəl
ˈwɔː.mɪŋ/
grow (v) /grəʊ/
headphones (n) /ˈhed.fəʊnz/
heavy (adj) /ˈhev.i/
helmet (n) /ˈhel.mət/
however (adv) /ˌhaʊˈev.ə/
human (adj) /ˈhjuː.mən/
hurricane (n) /ˈhʌr.ɪ.kən/
increase (n) /ˈɪn.kriːs/
individual (adj)
/ˌɪn.dɪˈvɪdʒ.u.əl/
instead (adv) /ɪnˈsted/
interact (v) /ˌɪn.tərˈækt/
interactive (adj)
/ˌɪn.tərˈæk.tɪv/
land (n) /lænd/
level (n) /ˈlev.əl/
life (n) /laɪf/
light bulb (n) /ˈlaɪt ˌbʌlb/
medical (adj) /ˈmed.ɪ.kəl/
memory (n) /ˈmem.ər.i/
need (v) /niːd/
need (v) /niːd/

neighbourhood (n)
/ˈneɪ.bə.hʊd/
office (n) /ˈɒf.ɪs/
oil (n) /ɔɪl/
optimist (n) /ˈɒp.tɪ.mɪst/
optimistic (adj) /ˌɒp.tɪˈmɪs.tɪk/
pain (n) /peɪn/
panel (n) /ˈpæn.əl/
pass (v) /pɑːs/
pessimistic (adj)
/ˌpes.ɪˈmɪs.tɪk/
pick up (v) /ˌpɪk ˈʌp/
plant (n) /plɑːnt/
point (n) /pɔɪnt/
pollution (n) /ˌpəˈluː.ʃən/
power (n) /ˈpaʊ.ə/
powerful (adj) /ˈpaʊ.ə.fəl/
produce (v) /prəˈdʒuːs/
promise (n) /ˈprɒm.ɪs/
purify (v) /ˈpjʊə.rɪ.faɪ/
real (adj) /rɪəl/
recycle (v) /riːˈsaɪ.kəl/
recycling (n) /riːˈsaɪ.klɪŋ/
refuge (n) /ˈref.juːdʒ/
remove (v) /rɪˈmuːv/
renewable (adj) /rɪˈnjuː.ə.bəl/
robot (n) /ˈrəʊ.bɒt/
roof (n) /ruːf/
safe (adj) /seɪf/
sea (n) /siː/
share (v) /ʃeə/
solar (adj) /ˈsəʊ.lə/
steak (n) /steɪk/
storm (n) /stɔːm/
substance (n) /ˈsʌb.stəns/
such (adj) /sʌtʃ/
suddenly (adv) /ˈsʌd.ən.li/
sun (n) /sʌn/
sunny (adj) /ˈsʌn.i/
tank (n) /tæŋk/
tap (n) /tæp/
temperature (n) /ˈtem.prɪ.tʃə/
thief (n) /θiːf/
torch (n) /tɔːtʃ/
translation (n) /ˌtrænzˈleɪ.ʃən/
turbine (n) /ˈtɜː.baɪn/
turn off (v) /ˌtɜːn ˈɒf/
typical (adj) /ˈtɪp.ɪ.kəl/
unhealthy (adj) /ʌnˈhel.θi/
university (n) /ˌjuː.nɪˈvɜː.sə.ti/
virtual reality (n) /ˌvɜː.tʃu.əl
riˈæl.ə.ti/
waste (n) /weɪst/
white board (n) /ˈwaɪt.bɔːd/
wireless (adj) /ˈwaɪə.ləs/
worm (n) /wɜːm/
worry (v) /ˈwʌr.i/

Unit 3

achieve (v) /əˈtʃiːv/
actually (adv) /ˈæk.tʃu.ə.li/
against (prep) /əˈgenst/
archery (n) /ˈɑː.tʃər.i/
avocado (n) /ˌæv.əˈkɑː.dəʊ/
award (n) /əˈwɔːd/
bronze (n) /brɒnz/

camel (n) /ˈkæm.əl/
camping (n) /ˈkæm.pɪŋ/
canoe (n) /kəˈnuː/
canoeing (n) /kəˈnuː.ɪŋ/
conditions (n) /kənˈdɪʃ.ənz/
cookery (n) /ˈkʊk.ər.i/
course (n) /kɔːs/
dark (n) /dɑːk/
develop (v) /dɪˈvel.əp/
difference (n) /ˈdɪf.ər.əns/
disabled (adj) /dɪˈseɪ.bəld/
dive (v) /daɪv/
diving (n) /ˈdaɪv.ɪŋ/
DJ (n) /ˈdiː.dʒeɪ/
edible (adj) /ˈed.ɪ.bəl/
effort (n) /ˈef.ət/
emergency (n) /iˈmɜː.dʒən.si/
essential (adj) /iˈsen.tʃəl/
exact (adj) /ɪgˈzækt/
exciting (adj) /ɪkˈsaɪ.tɪŋ/
expedition (n) /ek.spəˈdɪʃ.ən/
first aid (n) /ˌfɜːst ˈeɪd/
flu (n) /fluː/
go-karting (n) /ˈgəʊ ˌkɑː.tɪŋ/
gold (n) /gəʊld/
height (n) /haɪt/
helicopter (n) /ˈhel.ɪ.kɒp.tə/
hide (v) /haɪd/
hike (v) /haɪk/
hire (v) /haɪə/
hope (v) /həʊp/
horrible (adj) /ˈhɒr.ə.bəl/
horseback (n) /ˈhɔːs.bæk/
hostel (n) /ˈhɒs.təl/
imagine (v) /iˈmædʒ.ɪn/
improve (v) /ɪmˈpruːv/
insect (n) /ˈɪn.sekt/
international (adj)
/ɪn.təˈnæʃ.ən.əl/
journey (n) /ˈdʒɜː.ni/
junior (adj) /ˈdʒuː.ni.ə/
kayaking (n) /ˈkaɪ.æk.ɪŋ/
kit (n) /kɪt/
leaf (n) /liːf/
leaflet (n) /ˈliː.flət/
lifesaving (n) /ˈlaɪfˌseɪ.vɪŋ/
light (v) /laɪt/
map (n) /mæp/
martial art (n) /ˌmɑː.ʃəl ˈɑːt/
maximum (adj)
/ˈmæk.sɪ.məm/
meal (n) /miːl/
mean (v) /miːn/
meeting (n) /ˈmiː.tɪŋ/
mention (v) /ˈmen.ʃən/
minimum (adj) /ˈmɪn.ɪ.məm/
mountain (n) /ˈmaʊn.tɪn/
mushroom (n) /ˈmʌʃ.rʊm/
nature (n) /ˈneɪ.tʃə/
navigate (v) /ˈnæv.ɪ.geɪt/
normal (adj) /ˈnɔː.məl/
nothing (n) /ˈnʌθ.ɪŋ/
outback (n) /ˈaʊt.bæk/
perform (v) /pəˈfɔːm/
perhaps (adv) /pəˈhæps/
physical (adj) /ˈfɪz.ɪ.kəl/
pillow (n) /ˈpɪl.əʊ/

precise (adj) /prɪˈsaɪs/
presenter (n) /prɪˈzen.tə/
programme (n) /ˈprəʊ.græm/
pyramid (n) /ˈpɪr.ə.mɪd/
quiz (n) /kwɪz/
race (n) /reɪs/
raise (v) /reɪz/
recently (adv) /ˈriː.sənt.li/
record (v) /rɪˈkɔːd/
recreation (n) /re.kriˈeɪ.ʃən/
referee (n) /ref.ərˈiː/
relax (v) /rɪˈlæks/
repair (n) /rɪˈpeə/
repellent (n) /rɪˈpel.ənt/
reserve (v) /rɪˈzɜːv/
respect (v) /rɪˈspekt/
responsibility (n)
/rɪ.spɒn.səˈbɪl.ə.ti/
result (n) /rɪˈzʌlt/
risk (n) /rɪsk/
rock (n) /rɒk/
rollercoaster (n)
/ˈrəʊ.ləˌkəʊ.stə/
romantic (adj) /rəʊˈmæn.tɪk/
safely (adv) /ˈseɪf.li/
sauce (n) /sɔːs/
scheme (n) /skiːm/
scuba diving (n) /ˈskuː.bə
ˌdaɪv.ɪŋ/
section (n) /ˈsek.ʃən/
service (n) /ˈsɜː.vɪs/
shelter (n) /ˈʃel.tə/
silver (n) /ˈsɪl.və/
single (n) /ˈsɪŋ.gəl/
skate (v) /skeɪt/
skateboarding (n)
/ˈskeɪt.bɔːd.ɪŋ/
skiing (n) /ˈskiː.ɪŋ/
spicy (adj) /ˈspaɪ.si/
spirit (n) /ˈspɪr.ɪt/
stove (n) /stəʊv/
sun cream (n) /ˈsʌn ˌkriːm/
surf (v) /sɜːf/
surfing (n) /ˈsɜː.f.ɪŋ/
survival (n) /səˈvaɪ.vəl/
survive (v) /səˈvaɪv/
talented (adj) /ˈtæl.ən.tɪd/
theatre (n) /ˈθɪə.tə/
tortilla (n) /tɔːˈtiː.ə/
track (n) /træk/
trainer (n) /ˈtreɪn.ə/
trampolining (n)
/ˌtræm.pəˈliːn.ɪŋ/
trek (v) /trek/
trekking (n) /ˈtrek.ɪŋ/
try (v) /traɪ/
tutor (n) /ˈtʃuː.tə/
volunteer (n) /ˌvɒl.ənˈtɪə/
volunteering (n)
/ˌvɒl.ənˈtɪər.ɪŋ/
wild (n) /waɪld/
without (prep) /wɪˈðaʊt/

Unit 4

absolutely (adv) /ˌæb.səˈluːt.li/
admire (v) /ədˈmaɪə/

advertise *(v)* /ˈæd.və.taɪz/
agree *(v)* /əˈgriː/
annoy *(v)* /əˈnɔɪ/
anybody *(pron)* /ˈen.iˌbɒd.i/
anymore *(adv)* /ˌen.iˈmɔː/
anyone *(pron)* /ˈen.i.wʌn/
anywhere *(adv)* /ˈen.i.weə/
argument *(n)* /ˈɑːg.jə.mənt/
artist *(n)* /ˈɑː.tɪst/
baby *(n)* /ˈbeɪ.bi/
barbecue *(n)* /ˈbɑː.bɪ.kjuː/
beautiful *(adj)* /ˈbjuː.tɪ.fəl/
between *(prep)* /bɪˈtwiːn/
bill *(n)* /bɪl/
buy *(v)* /baɪ/
carefully *(adv)* /ˈkeə.fəl.i/
chain *(n)* /tʃeɪn/
channel *(n)* /ˈtʃæn.əl/
chill out *(v)* /ˌtʃɪl ˈaʊt/
combine *(v)* /kəmˈbaɪn/
complain *(v)* /kəmˈpleɪn/
concert *(n)* /ˈkɒn.sɜːt/
criticism *(n)* /ˈkrɪt.ɪ.sɪ.zəm/
cross *(v)* /krɒs/
dangerous *(adj)* /ˈdeɪn.dʒər.əs/
decoration *(n)* /dek.əˈreɪ.ʃən/
encourage *(v)* /ɪnˈkʌr.ɪdʒ/
enough *(adv)* /ɪˈnʌf/
everybody *(pron)* /ˈev.riˌbɒd.i/
everyone *(pron)* /ˈev.ri.wʌn/
everything *(pron)* /ˈev.ri.θɪŋ/
everywhere *(adv)* /ˈev.ri.weə/
exactly *(adv)* /ɪgˈzækt.li/
expect *(v)* /ɪkˈspekt/
expensive *(adj)* /ɪkˈspen.sɪv/
explanation *(n)* /ek.spləˈneɪ.ʃən/
fact *(n)* /fækt/
fair *(adj)* /feə/
fancy dress *(n)* /ˌfæn.si ˈdres/
few *(adj)* /fjuː/
freedom *(n)* /ˈfriː.dəm/
frustrated *(adj)* /frʌsˈtreɪt.ɪd/
gadget *(n)* /ˈgædʒ.ɪt/
gel *(n)* /dʒel/
glass *(n)* /glɑːs/
guest *(n)* /gest/
hang on *(v)* /ˈhæŋ ˌɒn/
hang out *(v)* /ˌhæŋ ˈaʊt/
hit *(n)* /hɪt/
hold *(v)* /həʊld/
hurry up *(v)* /ˌhʌr.i ˈʌp/
include *(v)* /ɪŋˈkluːd/
independent *(adj)* /ˌɪn.dɪˈpen.dənt/
jewellery *(n)* /ˈdʒuː.əl.ri/
journalist *(n)* /ˈdʒɜː.nə.lɪst/
just *(adv)* /dʒʌst/
marathon *(n)* /ˈmær.ə.θən/
market *(n)* /ˈmɑː.kɪt/
material *(n)* /məˈtɪə.ri.əl/
middle-aged *(adj)* /ˌmɪd.əlˈeɪdʒd/
model *(n)* /ˈmɒd.əl/
moody *(adj)* /ˈmuː.di/
muddy *(adj)* /ˈmʌd.i/

nobody *(pron)* /ˈnəʊ.bə.di/
nowadays *(adv)* /ˈnaʊ.ə.deɪz/
nowhere *(adv)* /ˈnəʊ.weə/
pill *(n)* /pɪl/
poor *(n)* /pɔː/
possibly *(adv)* /ˈpɒs.ə.bli/
poster *(n)* /ˈpəʊ.stə/
prepare *(v)* /prɪˈpeə/
pressure *(n)* /ˈpreʃ.ə/
pretty *(adj)* /ˈprɪt.i/
product *(n)* /ˈprɒd.ʌkt/
protest *(n)* /ˈprəʊ.test/
protester *(n)* /prəˈtest.ə/
recent *(adj)* /ˈriː.sənt/
recyclable *(adj)* /riːˈsaɪ.klə.bəl/
refuse *(v)* /rɪˈfjuːz/
relationship *(n)* /rɪˈleɪ.ʃən.ʃɪp/
remote control *(n)* /rɪˌməʊt kənˈtrəʊl/
request *(v)* /rɪˈkwest/
resist *(v)* /rɪˈzɪst/
resource *(n)* /rɪˈzɔːs/
rich *(n)* /rɪtʃ/
rob *(v)* /rɒb/
sell *(v)* /sel/
serious *(adj)* /ˈsɪə.ri.əs/
set up *(v)* /ˌset ˈʌp/
shampoo *(n)* /ʃæmˈpuː/
shop *(v)* /ʃɒp/
shopping centre *(n)* /ˈʃɒp.ɪŋ ˌsen.tə/
somebody *(pron)* /ˈsʌm.bə.di/
someone *(pron)* /ˈsʌm.wʌn/
somewhere *(adv)* /ˈsʌm.weə/
soon *(adv)* /suːn/
sort out *(v)* /ˌsɔːt ˈaʊt/
specific *(adj)* /spəˈsɪf.ɪk/
spread *(v)* /spred/
stall *(n)* /stɔːl/
stress *(n)* /stres/
stressed *(adj)* /strest/
stressful *(adj)* /ˈstres.fəl/
strict *(adj)* /strɪkt/
surely *(adv)* /ˈʃɔː.li/
swap *(v)* /swɒp/
toddler *(n)* /ˈtɒd.lə/
top *(n)* /tɒp/
traffic *(n)* /ˈtræf.ɪk/
tray *(n)* /treɪ/
treat *(v)* /triːt/
twice *(adv)* /twaɪs/
vitamin *(n)* /ˈvɪt.ə.mɪn/
yet *(adv)* /jet/
zombie *(n)* /ˈzɒm.bi/

Unit 5

access *(n)* /ˈæk.ses/
ache *(n)* /eɪk/
aftershock *(n)* /ˈɑːf.tə.ʃɒk/
agreement *(n)* /əˈgriː.mənt/
alert *(adj)* /əˈlɜːt/
almost *(adv)* /ˈɔːl.məʊst/
alone *(adv)* /əˈləʊn/
along *(prep)* /əˈlɒŋ/

annoying *(adj)* /əˈnɔɪ.ɪŋ/
apologise *(v)* /əˈpɒl.ə.dʒaɪz/
autograph *(v)* /ˈɔː.tə.grɑːf/
basic *(adj)* /ˈbeɪ.sɪk/
beat *(v)* /biːt/
behaviour *(n)* /bɪˈheɪ.vjə/
block *(v)* /blɒk/
boil *(v)* /bɔɪl/
bookcase *(n)* /ˈbʊk.keɪs/
break *(v)* /breɪk/
breathe *(v)* /briːð/
bully *(n)* /ˈbʊl.i/
bully *(v)* /ˈbʊl.i/
burn *(v)* /bɜːn/
caller *(n)* /ˈkɔː.lə/
canteen *(n)* /kænˈtiːn/
capital *(n)* /ˈkæp.ɪ.təl/
care *(v)* /keə/
chance *(n)* /tʃɑːns/
childhood *(n)* /ˈtʃaɪld.hʊd/
clearly *(adv)* /ˈklɪə.li/
comfortable *(adj)* /ˈkʌmf.tə.bəl/
company *(n)* /ˈkʌm.pə.ni/
concentrate *(v)* /ˈkɒn.sən.treɪt/
cough *(n)* /kɒf/
culture *(n)* /ˈkʌl.tʃə/
cut *(v)* /kʌt/
damage *(v)* /ˈdæm.ɪdʒ/
delicious *(adj)* /dɪˈlɪʃ.əs/
depressed *(adj)* /dɪˈprest/
die *(v)* /daɪ/
doctor *(n)* /ˈdɒk.tə/
drop *(v)* /drɒp/
dump *(n)* /dʌmp/
earache *(n)* /ˈɪə.reɪk/
earthquake *(n)* /ˈɜːθ.kweɪk/
explain *(v)* /ɪkˈspleɪn/
explosion *(n)* /ɪkˈspləʊ.ʒən/
fail *(v)* /feɪl/
fault *(n)* /fɔːlt/
feather *(n)* /ˈfeð.ə/
fight *(v)* /faɪt/
fine *(adj)* /faɪn/
firstly *(adv)* /ˈfɜːst.li/
freely *(adv)* /ˈfriː.li/
freeze *(v)* /friːz/
friendly *(adj)* /ˈfrend.li/
frightened *(adj)* /ˈfraɪ.tənd/
frightening *(adj)* /ˈfraɪ.tən.ɪŋ/
gas *(n)* /gæs/
headache *(n)* /ˈhed.eɪk/
heat *(n)* /hiːt/
helpline *(n)* /ˈhelp.laɪn/
hurt *(v)* /hɜːt/
ignore *(v)* /ɪgˈnɔː/
ill *(adj)* /ɪl/
illness *(n)* /ˈɪl.nəs/
impress *(v)* /ɪmˈpres/
indoors *(adv)* /ɪnˈdɔːz/
injury *(n)* /ˈɪn.dʒər.i/
instruction *(n)* /ɪnˈstrʌk.ʃən/
internet *(n)* /ˈɪn.tə.net/
let *(v)* /let/
lie *(n)* /laɪ/
lift *(n)* /lɪft/

lonely *(adj)* /ˈləʊn.li/
matter *(v)* /ˈmæt.ə/
mechanic *(n)* /mɪˈkæn.ɪk/
medicine *(n)* /ˈmed.sən/
mind *(v)* /maɪnd/
mix *(v)* /mɪks/
multiply *(v)* /ˈmʌl.tɪ.plaɪ/
nasty *(adj)* /ˈnɑː.sti/
nationality *(n)* /ˌnæʃ.ənˈæl.ə.ti/
obvious *(adj)* /ˈɒb.vi.əs/
operation *(n)* /ˌɒp.ərˈeɪ.ʃən/
outdoors *(adv)* /aʊtˈdɔːz/
oxygen *(n)* /ˈɒk.sɪ.dʒən/
permission *(n)* /pəˈmɪʃ.ən/
pocket money *(n)* /ˈpɒk.ɪt ˌmʌn.i/
polio *(n)* /ˈpəʊ.li.əʊ/
possession *(n)* /pəˈzeʃ.ən/
possible *(adj)* /ˈpɒs.ə.bəl/
prefer *(v)* /prɪˈfɜː/
properly *(adv)* /ˈprɒp.əl.i/
protect *(v)* /prəˈtekt/
provider *(n)* /prəˈvaɪ.də/
quake *(n)* /kweɪk/
relaxing *(adj)* /rɪˈlæks.ɪŋ/
religion *(n)* /rɪˈlɪdʒ.ən/
remember *(v)* /rɪˈmem.bə/
repair *(v)* /rɪˈpeə/
report *(v)* /rɪˈpɔːt/
revise *(v)* /rɪˈvaɪz/
rude *(adj)* /ruːd/
safety *(n)* /ˈseɪf.ti/
secondly *(adv)* /ˈsek.ənd.li/
sick *(adj)* /sɪk/
site *(n)* /saɪt/
six-year-old *(adj)* /ˈsɪks.jɪərˌəʊld/
skin *(n)* /skɪn/
social *(adj)* /ˈsəʊ.ʃəl/
sore *(adj)* /sɔː/
starve *(v)* /stɑːv/
stomach *(n)* /ˈstʌm.ək/
switch *(n)* /swɪtʃ/
taste *(v)* /teɪst/
throat *(n)* /θrəʊt/
thumb *(n)* /θʌm/
toothache *(n)* /ˈtuːθ.eɪk/
trust *(v)* /trʌst/
tuna *(n)* /ˈtʃuː.nə/
unfortunately *(adv)* /ʌnˈfɔː.tʃən.ət.li/
unhappy *(adj)* /ʌnˈhæp.i/
vaccination *(n)* /ˌvæk.sɪˈneɪ.ʃən/
victim *(n)* /ˈvɪk.tɪm/
weightlifting *(n)* /ˈweɪtˌlɪf.tɪŋ/

Unit 6

ambition *(n)* /æmˈbɪʃ.ən/
animation *(n)* /ˌæn.ɪˈmeɪ.ʃən/
appear *(v)* /əˈpɪə/
appearance *(n)* /əˈpɪə.rəns/
artistic *(adj)* /ɑːˈtɪs.tɪk/
audience *(n)* /ˈɔː.di.əns/
caravan *(n)* /ˈkær.ə.væn/

career (n) /kə'rɪə/
caterer (n) /'keɪ.tər.ə/
catering (n) /'keɪ.tər.ɪŋ/
cheerful (n) /'tʃɪə.fəl/
comedy (n) /'kɒm.ə.di/
complete (v) /kəm'pliːt/
contestant (n) /kən'tes.tənt/
creature (n) /'kriː.tʃə/
credit (n) /'kred.ɪt/
crocodile (n) /'krɒk.ə.daɪl/
daily (adj) /'deɪ.li/
depend (v) /dɪ'pend/
detail (n) /'diː.teɪl/
direct (v) /daɪ'rekt/
director (n) /daɪ'rek.tə/
during (prep) /'djʊə.rɪŋ/
editor (n) /'ed.ɪ.tə/
effect (n) /ɪ'fekt/
equipment (n) /ɪ'kwɪp.mənt/
extra (n) /'ek.strə/
fan (n) /fæn/
favourite (adj) /'feɪ.vər.ɪt/
fear (n) /fɪə/
film (v) /fɪlm/
final (n) /'faɪ.nəl/
finalist (n) /'faɪ.nəl.ɪst/
finally (adv) /'faɪ.nəli/
futuristic (adj) /ˌfjuː.tʃə'rɪs.tɪk/
graphics (n) /'græf.ɪks/
historical (adj) /hɪ'stɒr.ɪkəl/
horror (n) /'hɒr.ə/
identify (v) /aɪ'den.tɪ.faɪ/
incredibly (adv) /ɪn'kred.ə.bli/
industry (n) /'ɪn.də.stri/
inside (adj) /ɪn'saɪd/
interested (adj) /'ɪn.trəst.ɪd/
interpret (v) /ɪn'tɜː.prɪt/
judge (n) /dʒʌdʒ/
limitation (n) /lɪm.ɪ'teɪ.ʃən/
listener (n) /'lɪs.nə/
location (n) /ləʊ'keɪ.ʃən/
look forward to (v) /ˌlʊk
    'fɔː.wəd tuː/
maker (n) /'meɪ.kə/
make-up (n) /'meɪk.ʌp/
mechanical (adj)
    /mɪ'kæn.ɪkəl/
mine (pron) /maɪn/
modern (adj) /'mɒd.ən/
monster (n) /'mɒn.stə/
movie (n) /'muː.vi/
nervous (adj) /'nɜː.vəs/
omit (v) /əʊ'mɪt/
performance (n) /pə'fɔː.məns/
performer (n) /pə'fɔː.mə/
plot (n) /plɒt/
practical (adj) /'præk.tɪ.kəl/
private (adj) /'praɪ.vɪt/
prize (n) /praɪz/
producer (n) /prə'djuː.sə/
professional (adj)
    /prə'feʃ.ən.əl/
prop (n) /prɒp/
qualification (n)
    /ˌkwɒl.ɪ.fɪ'keɪ.ʃən/
rafting (n) /'rɑːf.tɪŋ/
realistic (adj) /rɪə'lɪs.tɪk/

recognise (v) /'rek.əg.naɪz/
recordist (n) /rɪ'kɔː.dɪst/
rehearse (v) /rɪ'hɜːs/
runner (n) /'rʌn.ə/
runway (n) /'rʌn.weɪ/
scene (n) /siːn/
script (n) /skrɪpt/
scriptwriter (n) /'skrɪpt.raɪ.tə/
secret (adj) /'siː.krət/
security (n) /sɪ'kjʊə.rə.ti/
sensation (n) /sen'seɪ.ʃən/
serve (v) /sɜːv/
specialise (v) /'speʃ.əl.aɪz/
sportsperson (n)
    /'spɔːts.pɜː.sən/
staff (n) /stɑːf/
stage (n) /steɪdʒ/
steward (n) /'stjuː.əd/
studio (n) /'stjuː.di.əʊ/
stunt (n) /stʌnt/
support (n) /sə'pɔːt/
thought (n) /θɔːt/
transport (v) /træn'spɔːt/
truck (n) /trʌk/
viewer (n) /vjuːə/
visual (adj) /'vɪʒ.u.əl/
voice (n) /vɔɪs/
vote (n) /vəʊt/
waste (v) /weɪst/

Unit 7

aim (n) /eɪm/
attack (v) /ə'tæk/
ban (v) /bæn/
builder (n) /'bɪl.də/
burglar (n) /'bɜː.glə/
can opener (n) /'kæn
    ˌəʊ.pənə/
concern (n) /kən'sɜːn/
concerned (adj) /kən'sɜːnd/
conductor (n) /kən'dʌk.tə/
cooker (n) /'kʊk.ə/
council (n) /'kaʊn.səl/
crime (n) /kraɪm/
criminal (n) /'krɪm.ɪ.nəl/
cultural (adj) /'kʌl.tʃər.əl/
cure (n) /kjʊə/
detective (n) /dɪ'tek.tɪv/
disease (n) /dɪ'ziːz/
dishwasher (n) /'dɪʃ.wɒʃ.ə/
elect (v) /i'lekt/
endangered (adj)
    /ɪn'deɪn.dʒəd/
facilities (n) /fə'sɪl.ə.tiz/
fence (n) /fens/
get rid of (v) /ˌget 'rɪd.əv/
government (n) /'gʌv.ən.mənt/
habit (n) /'hæb.ɪt/
honest (adj) /'ɒn.ɪst/
imaginary (adj)
    /ɪ'mædʒ.ɪ.nər.i/
impact (n) /'ɪm.pækt/
improvement (n)
    /ɪm'pruːv.mənt/
keep (v) /kiːp/
law (n) /lɔː/

lawn mower (n) /'lɔːn ˌməʊə/
leader (n) /'liː.də/
litter (n) /'lɪt.ə/
local (adj) /'ləʊ.kəl/
millionaire (n) /ˌmɪl.jə'neə/
mugger (n) /'mʌg.ə/
peace (n) /piːs/
pickpocket (n) /'pɪk.pɒk.ɪt/
plant (v) /plɑːnt/
politics (n) /'pɒl.ə.tɪks/
poverty (n) /'pɒv.ə.ti/
pretend (v) /prɪ'tend/
printer (n) /'prɪn.tə/
property (n) /'prɒp.ə.ti/
public (adj) /'pʌb.lɪk/
regular (adj) /'reg.jə.lə/
separate (adj) /'sep.ər.ət/
seriously (adv) /'sɪə.ri.əs.li/
shoplifter (n) /'ʃɒp.lɪf.tə/
society (n) /sə'saɪ.ə.ti/
species (n) /'spiː.ʃiːz/
stapler (n) /'steɪ.plə/
state school (n) /'steɪt ˌskuːl/
steel band (n) /ˌstiːl 'bænd/
strange (adj) /streɪndʒ/
style (n) /staɪl/
suffering (n) /'sʌfər.ɪŋ/
tarantula (n) /tə'ræn.tʃə.lə/
toaster (n) /'təʊs.tə/
tolerance (n) /'tɒl.ər.əns/
truth (n) /truːθ/
type (n) /taɪp/
UFO (n) /ˌjuː.ef'əʊ/
unfit (adj) /ʌn'fɪt/
uniform (n) /'juː.nɪ.fɔːm/
upset (v) /ʌp'set/
value (n) /'væl.juː/
vandal (n) /'væn.dəl/
violence (n) /'vaɪ.ə.ləns/
vote (v) /vəʊt/
wallet (n) /'wɒl.ɪt/

Unit 8

able (adj) /'eɪ.bəl/
above (prep) /ə'bʌv/
advance (n) /əd'vɑːns/
alligator (n) /'æl.ɪ.geɪ.tə/
aloud (adv) /ə'laʊd/
aluminium (n) /ˌæl.
    jə'mɪn.i.əm/
amongst (prep) /ə'mʌŋst/
anger (n) /'æŋ.gə/
anonymous (adj)
    /ə'nɒn.ɪ.məs/
apostrophe (n) /ə'pɒs.trə.fi/
arrest (v) /ə'rest/
bar (n) /bɑː/
bare (adj) /beə/
bee (n) /biː/
blind (adj) /blaɪnd/
blogger (n) /'blɒg.ə/
bow (v) /baʊ/
butterfly (n) /'bʌt.ə.flaɪ/
code (n) /kəʊd/
coin (n) /kɔɪn/
colon (n) /'kəʊl.ɒn/

coloured (adj) /'kʌl.əd/
comic (n) /'kɒm.ɪk/
comma (n) /'kɒm.ə/
communicate (v)
    /kə'mjuː.nɪ.keɪt/
contest (n) /'kɒn.test/
counter (n) /'kaʊn.tə/
cricket (n) /'krɪk.ɪt/
cyberbullying (n)
    /'saɪ.bəˌbʊli.ɪŋ/
dash (n) /dæʃ/
delicatessen (n)
    /ˌdel.ɪ.kə'tes.ən/
deliver (v) /dɪ'lɪv.ə/
dictate (v) /dɪk'teɪt/
discover (v) /dɪ'skʌv.ə/
disgust (n) /dɪs'gʌst/
distance (n) /'dɪs.təns/
diver (n) /'daɪ.və/
dot (v) /dɒt/
emotion (n) /ɪ'məʊ.ʃən/
engineer (n) /en.dʒɪ'nɪə/
enthusiastic (adj)
    /ɪn.θjuː.zi'æs.tɪk/
exchange (v) /ɪks'tʃeɪndʒ/
exclamation mark (n)
    /ˌeks.klə'meɪ.ʃən ˌmɑːk/
file (n) /faɪl/
flag (n) /flæg/
force (v) /fɔːs/
freezing (adj) /'friː.zɪŋ/
fresh (adj) /freʃ/
frog (n) /frɒg/
gate (n) /geɪt/
gesture (n) /'dʒes.tʃə/
greet (v) /griːt/
greeting (n) /'griː.tɪŋ/
happiness (n) /'hæp.ɪ.nɪs/
hug (v) /hʌg/
human (n) /'hjuː.mən/
hyphen (n) /'haɪ.fən/
ingredient (n) /ɪn'griː.di.ənt/
kiss (v) /kɪs/
land (v) /lænd/
letter (n) /'let.ə/
list (v) /lɪst/
melt (v) /melt/
meteorite (n) /'miː.ti.ər.aɪt/
Morse code (n) /ˌmɔːs 'kəʊd/
nod (v) /nɒd/
non-verbal (adj) /ˌnɒn'vɜː.bəl/
organise (v) /'ɔː.gən.aɪz/
outer space (n) /ˌaʊ.tə 'speɪs/
peacock (n) /'piː.kɒk/
penguin (n) /'peŋ.gwɪn/
poetry (n) /'pəʊ.ə.tri/
point (v) /pɔɪnt/
police (n) /pə'liːs/
post (v) /pəʊst/
postal (adj) /'pəʊ.stəl/
postcard (n) /'pəʊst.kɑːd/
print (v) /prɪnt/
printing press (n)
    /'prɪnt.ɪŋ ˌpres/
process (n) /'prəʊ.ses/
repeat (v) /rɪ'piːt/
rescue (v) /'res.kjuː/

roll *(v)* /rəʊl/
rub *(v)* /rʌb/
sadness *(n)* /'sæd.nəs/
salad *(n)* /'sæl.əd/
seafood *(n)* /'siː.fuːd/
separate *(v)* /'sep.ər.eɪt/
shake *(v)* /ʃeɪk/
sheet *(n)* /ʃiːt/
sole *(n)* /səʊl/
South Pole *(n)* /ˌsaʊθ 'pəʊl/
spot *(n)* /spɒt/
store *(n)* /stɔː/
system *(n)* /'sɪs.təm/
tail *(n)* /teɪl/
tame *(adj)* /teɪm/
thirdly *(adv)* /'θɜːd.li/
tiny *(adj)* /'taɪ.ni/
ton *(n)* /tʌn/
touch *(v)* /tʌtʃ/
tourist *(n)* /'tʊə.rɪst/
universal *(adj)* /ˌjuː.nɪ'vɜː.səl/
upset *(adj)* /ʌp'set/
vary *(v)* /'veə.ri/
video recorder *(n)* /'vɪd.i.əʊ. rɪˌkɔː.də/
video tape *(n)* /'vɪd.i.əʊ ˌteɪp/
visitor *(n)* /'vɪz.ɪ.tə/
wave *(v)* /weɪv/
whale *(n)* /weɪl/
wheel *(n)* /wiːl/
whose *(det)* /huːz/
wing *(n)* /wɪŋ/
worth *(n)* /wɜːθ/
X-ray *(n)* /'eks.reɪ/

Unit 9

atmosphere *(n)* /'æt.məs.fɪə/
belong *(v)* /bɪ'lɒŋ/
bet *(v)* /bet/
cable car *(n)* /'keɪ.bəl kɑː/
castle *(n)* /'kɑː.səl/
clown *(n)* /klaʊn/
coast *(n)* /kəʊst/
crowded *(adj)* /'kraʊd.ɪd/
dirt *(n)* /dɜːt/
entertainment *(n)* /ˌen.tə'teɪn.mənt/
gallery *(n)* /'gæl.ər.i/
golf *(n)* /gɒlf/
juggler *(n)* /'dʒʌg.lə/
magician *(n)* /mə'dʒɪʃ.ən/
mainly *(adv)* /'meɪn.li/
mall *(n)* /mæl/
megacity *(n)* /'meg.ə.sɪ.ti/
monkey *(n)* /'mʌŋ.ki/
muffin *(n)* /'mʌf.ɪn/
narrow *(adj)* /'nær.əʊ/
nearly *(adv)* /'nɪə.li/
popular *(adj)* /'pɒp.jə.lə/
population *(n)* /pɒp.jə'leɪ.ʃən/
refer *(v)* /rɪ'fɜː/
reporter *(n)* /rɪ'pɔː.tə/
research *(n)* /rɪ'sɜːtʃ/
sights *(n)* /saɪts/
sightseeing *(n)* /'saɪt.siː.ɪŋ/
similar *(adj)* /'sɪm.ɪ.lə/
skyline *(n)* /'skaɪ.laɪn/

smell *(n)* /smel/
smoothie *(n)* /'smuː.ði/
sometime *(adv)* /'sʌm.taɪm/
stormy *(adj)* /'stɔː.mi/
suburb *(n)* /'sʌb.ɜːb/
suffer *(v)* /'sʌf.ə/
sure *(adj)* /ʃɔː/
treatment *(n)* /'triːt.mənt/
trick *(n)* /trɪk/
unsure *(adj)* /ʌn'ʃɔː/
village *(n)* /'vɪl.ɪdʒ/
waterfront *(n)* /'wɔː.tə.frʌnt/

Unit 10

allowance *(n)* /ə'laʊ.əns/
apartment *(n)* /ə'pɑːt.mənt/
autobiography *(n)* /ɔː.tə.baɪ'ɒg.rə.fi/
ballet *(n)* /'bæl.eɪ/
biography *(n)* /baɪ'ɒg.rə.fi/
break-dancing *(n)* /'breɪk,dɑːn.sɪŋ/
bunch *(n)* /bʌntʃ/
cassette *(n)* /kə'set/
chore *(n)* /tʃɔː/
choreograph *(v)* /'kɒr.i.ə.grɑːf/
colourful *(adj)* /'kʌl.ə.fəl/
contact *(v)* /'kɒn.tækt/
countryside *(n)* /'kʌn.tri.saɪd/
dancer *(n)* /'dɑːn.sə/
determined *(adj)* /dɪ'tɜː.mɪnd/
discipline *(n)* /'dɪs.ə.plɪn/

fountain pen *(n)* /'faʊn.tən ˌpen/
guide book *(n)* /'gaɪd.bʊk/
pack *(v)* /pæk/
painful *(adj)* /'peɪn.fəl/
passport *(n)* /'pɑːs.pɔːt/
personality *(n)* /ˌpɜː.sən'æl.ə.ti/
phone box *(n)* /'fəʊn ˌbɒks/
pistol *(n)* /'pɪs.təl/
principal *(n)* /'prɪn.sɪ.pəl/
publish *(v)* /'pʌb.lɪʃ/
reach *(v)* /riːtʃ/
ready *(adj)* /'red.i/
reply *(v)* /rɪ'plaɪ/
scientific *(adj)* /ˌsaɪ.ən'tɪf.ɪk/
sci-fi *(n)* /'saɪ.faɪ/
size *(n)* /saɪz/
successful *(adj)* /sək'ses.fəl/
superstar *(n)* /'suː.pə.stɑː/
technology *(n)* /tek'nɒl.ə.dʒi/
teddy bear *(n)* /'ted.i beə/
toss *(v)* /tɒs/
tough *(adj)* /tʌf/
typewriter *(n)* /'taɪp,raɪ.tə/
volcano *(n)* /vɒl'keɪ.nəʊ/
world-famous *(adj)* /ˌwɜːld'feɪ.məs/

Phonetic symbols

Consonants

/p/	pen	/m/	make	/j/	you			
/b/	be	/n/	nice	/h/	he			
/t/	two	/ŋ/	sing	/θ/	thing			
/d/	do	/s/	see	/ð/	this			
/k/	can	/z/	trousers	/ʃ/	she			
/g/	good	/w/	we	/tʃ/	cheese			
/f/	five	/l/	listen	/ʒ/	usually			
/v/	very	/r/	right	/dʒ/	German			

Vowels

/æ/	man	/iː/	see
/ɑː/	father	/ʊ/	book
/e/	ten	/uː/	food
/ɜː/	thirteen	/ʌ/	up
/ə/	mother	/ɒ/	hot
/ɪ/	sit	/ɔː/	four

Diphthongs

/eɪ/	great	/eə/	chair
/aɪ/	fine	/aʊ/	town
/ɔɪ/	boy	/əʊ/	go
/ɪə/	hear	/ʊə/	pure

Thanks and Acknowledgements

The authors and publishers would like to thank the teachers who commented on the material at different stages of its development, the teachers who allowed us to observe their classes, and those who gave up their valuable time for interviews and focus groups.

The authors would like to thank all the people who have worked so hard on *Your Space*. We are especially grateful to James Dingle for inviting us to write this project and for his support during all stages of its development. We would also like to thank Frances Amrani, commissioning editor, and the editors Claire Powell, Rosemary Bradley and Ruth Bell-Pellegrini for their skilled editorial contributions, perceptive editing, and commitment to the project; the design team at Wild Apple; David Lawton for his design ideas; Emma Szlachta for her excellent project management and Graham Avery, production manager, for his support. We are grateful to all the other writers on the project for their creative input. We would also like to thank the many reviewers and teachers who contributed to the development of this course. We extend a special thank you to the editor Rachael Gibbon for her unwavering focus during the development process.

The publishers acknowledge the following sources of copyright material and are grateful for the permissions granted. While every effort has been made, it has not always been possible to identify the sources of all the material used, or to trace all copyright holders. If any omissions are brought to our notice, we will be happy to include the appropriate acknowledgements on reprinting.

The authors and publishers acknowledge the following sources of photographs and are grateful for the permissions granted.

p. 9 Thinkstock/Comstock Images; p. 10 Duncan Bryceland/Rex Features; p. 11 Anatoliy Samara/ Shutterstock; p. 18 NASA/Science Photo Library; p. 19 kriangkrai wangjai/Shutterstock; p. 23 (1) Alena Brozova/Shutterstock; p. 23 (2) Etunimet/ Shutterstock; p. 23 (3) Tatiana Trifan/Shutterstock; p. 23 (4) Kasra/Shutterstock; p. 23 (5) Andrew Buchin/Shutterstock; p. 23 (6) Abel Tumik/ Shutterstock; p. 23 (7) Slobo Mitic/iStock; p. 23 (8) Rtimages/iStock; p. 23 (9) Mark Herreid/ iStock; p. 23 (10) sinankocasian/iStock; p. 24 Thinkstock/Comstock Images; p. 25 Glyn Kirk/ Action Plus; p. 26 Action Images/Craig Brough; p. 26 imago sportfotodienst/Action Plus; p. 26 Action Images/Michael Regan Livepic; p. 27 Thinkstock; p. 30 Thinkstock/George Doyle; p. 31 (1) Yuri Arcurs/Shutterstock; p. 31 (2) Denise Fortado/Shutterstock; p. 31 (3) Suzanne Tucker/ Shutterstock; p. 31 (4) Tjerrie Smit/Shutterstock; p. 31 (5) Lucien Coman/Shutterstock; p. 31 (6) Melissa King/Shutterstock; p. 33t HadK/ Shutterstock; p. 33b upthebanner/Shutterstock; p. 34 Thinkstok/Comstock Images ; p. 35 Jupiterimages/Thinkstock; p. 37 JCElv/Sutterstock; p. 40l Trinity Mirror/Mirrorpix/Alamy; p. 40r Susan Law Cain/Shutterstock; p. 42 SVLumagraphica/ istock; p. 43bl Graeme Dawes/Shutterstock; p. 43tr Digital Vision/Thinkstock; p. 43br aodaodaodaod/ Shutterstock; p. 44 Dan Kenyon/Corbis; p. 46 Thinkstock; p. 46 Thinkstock; p. 46 Thinkstock; p. 48 Action Images/Henry Browne Livepic; p. 50t Stephane Cardinale/People Avenue/Corbis; p. 50b Ron Batzdorff/Warner Bros/Bureau L.A. Collections/ Corbis; p. 51t (1 & 5) Rune Hellestad/Corbis; p. 51t (2) Ken McKay/Rex Features; p. 51t (3) Frank Trapper/Corbis; p. 51t (4) Getty Images/Wirelmage; p. 51b Twentieth Century-Fox Film Corporation/The Kobal Collection; p. 54 Pete Salouto/Shutterstock; p. 55tl Jaime Duplass/iStock; p. 55tr Aldo Murillo/ iStock; p. 55cl Bill Noll/iStock; p. 55cr, br Monkey Business Images/Shutterstock; p. 55bl Jane/iStock; p. 58l Lisa F. Young/Shutterstock; p. 58r Catchlight Visual Services/Alamy; p. 59 Hung Chung Chih/ Shutterstock; p. 61 The Photographic Unit, Cambridge University Press; p. 62 Tim Denison/ iStockphoto; p. 64tr Thinkstock; p. 64 (1) SSPL via Getty Images; p. 64 (2) Byron Company (fl. 1890-1942)/© Museum of the City of New York, USA/The Bridgeman Art Library; p. 64 (3) Royal Astronomical Society/Science Photo Library; p. 64 (4) Mary Evans Picture Library; p. 64 (5) Fotolia/Mathew Antonino; p. 64 (6) Brenda Carson/Shutterstock; p. 67 Lukiyanova Natalia/frenta/Shutterstock; p. 70 Getty Images/Thinkstock; p. 74l iStockphoto/Thinkstock; p. 74r Thinkstock; p. 75 Ivan Bastien/iStockphoto; p. 77 Rido/Shutterstock; p. 80 Richard Gardner/Rex Features; p. 83 World History Archive/Alamy

Artwork Acknowledgements:

Adrian Barclay (*Beehive Illustration*) pp. 5, 32, 35, 38; Andrew Hennessey pp. 29, 56T, 69, 70, 77; Andy Parker pp. 73T, 75; Clive Goodyer pp. 6; David Benham (*Graham Cameron Illustration*) pp. 4, 15, 31B, 57T, 61, 66; Kate Rochester (Pickled Ink) pp. 12, 16, 20, 28, 35, 76, 78; Kevin Hopgoon p. 53; Laszlo Veres (*Beehive Illustration*) pp 47, 71, 83; Martin Bustamante (*Advocate Art*) pp. 13, 31T, 68, 72, 82; Nick Kobyluch (*New Division*) pp. 21, 45, 67; Peter Richardson pp. 9, 17, 25, 41, 49B, 57B, 65, 73B, 81B; Rory Walker pp. 8, 81T; Simon Rumble (*Beehive Illustration*) pp. 39, 49T; Tony Forbes p. 36; Wild Apple Design p. 59(leaves);

The publishers would like to extend a warm thanks to all the teachers and freelance collaborators who have made a valuable contribution to this material.